THE ART OF LEADING CIRCLE

HOW TO FILL, LEAD & GROW A WOMEN'S CIRCLE

SISTERSHIP CIRCLE

Copyright © 2020 by Tanya Lynn

All rights reserved. No part of this publication may be reproduced, distributed, or transmitted in any form or by any means, including photocopying, recording, or other electronic or mechanical methods, without the prior written permission of the publisher, except in the case of brief quotations embodied in critical reviews and certain other noncommercial uses permitted by copyright law. For permission requests, write to the publisher, addressed "Attention: Permissions Coordinator," at the address below.

ISBN: 978-1-7351169-0-7

New Fem Publishing

email: admin@sistershipcircle.com

www.sistershipcircle.com

Cover Design: Yana Nazarenko

Ordering Information:
Quantity sales. Special discounts are available on quantity purchases by corporations, associations, and others. For details, contact the publisher at the address above.

Praise for The Art of Leading Circle

"The Art of Leading Circle plays an important role in the evolution of humanity. In a world increasingly reliant on the internet, we need to build local communities for that connection that feeds our hearts and souls. This book will help us create more spaces where we can connect in the flesh to satisfy that basic human need and help us feel that sense of belonging that makes us one human family."
~ HeatherAsh Amara, author of *Warrior Goddess Training*

"Tanya is a fierce torchbearer for the divine feminine rising through sacred circle. Her devotion is apparent in the pages of this book. She's leading a circle movement that will change the world and every woman who wants to become a facilitator should read The Art of Leading Circle."
~ Christine Hassler, Master Coach, Podcast Host and author of *Expectation Hangover*

"The Art of Leading Circle is an essential guidebook, revealing Tanya's deep wisdom and extensive experience in leading powerful, connected and welcoming circles. Her 'circle technology' has had, and continues to have, global impact and implications as we upgrade our understanding of how to come together more consciously in this post-pandemic era."
~ Dr. Saida Désilets, Author, Tedx Speaker & Founder of the Global Sovereignty Initiative

THE ART OF LEADING CIRCLE

"I literally opened this book and thought: thank you, universe! Tanya has created an essential book for every woman who leads. There's so much juice here, from understanding that your circle needs both a masculine container and a feminine flow to an abundance of essential information on filling your circles and maintaining momentum. We are in a time when doing life together matters more than ever and especially for women, who thrive with sisterhood. It may sound easy to lead a women's circle, but having trained many brilliant women I've learned that people need to know how to lead circles. This book is like an all-in-one book that covers it all, and it's written with Tanya's deep knowledge, commitment and integrity to women's health and empowerment."

~ Karen Brody, author of *Daring to Rest*

"This book is a thorough step by step guide for any woman who wants to bring to life a sacred circle. And we need it! Women are looking for sisterhood more than ever, tired of being disconnected and isolated from each other."

~ Hemalayaa Behl, creator of *Embody Oracle Card Deck*

"The Art of Leading Circle is a MUST read for any woman on the path of women's leadership to embody the feminine principles and create safe, sacred space for connection and support."

~ Sofiah Thom, founder of Temple Body Arts School for Embodied Feminine Leadership

"Tanya is a fierce and passionate torchbearer for sisterhood. She's a genius at galvanizing women, not just to take their seat in the circle, but to step into the creation, facilitation and leadership of this ancient and most sacred of spaces. "

~ Lisa Schrader, founder Awakening Shakti

PRAISE FOR THE ART OF LEADING CIRCLE

"The Art of Leading Circle helps women step into their divine purpose in empowering women through gathering in circle for connection, support and celebration of the divine feminine. It's the only book I know out there of it's caliber, providing practical steps as well as the energetics."

~ Lisa Michaels, founder NaturCentrc

"Tanya is a fierce leader for the divine feminine rising through sacred circle. Her devotion is apparent in the pages of this book. She's leading a circle movement — with the goal of 1 million circles globally — that will change the world. Every woman who wants to be a part of this movement should become a facilitator and read The Art of Leading Circle."

~ Kenlyn Kolleen, author of *The Art of Turning 50* and Divine Feminine Summit host

"The Art of Leading Circle holds the keys for the modern priestess to unlock her leadership and service by bringing wombyn back to their divine feminine power through the ancient art and sacred medicine of circle and sisterhood."

~ Syma Kharal, Sacred Feminine teacher, #1 Bestselling author of *Goddess Reclaimed*

"I've been leading women's circles for the last twenty years, and I can tell you that Tanya is the real deal and this book is a must-have for anyone wanting to learn how to lead women's circles. It's heartful, insightful and a great step by step for meaningful gatherings."

~ Joanna Lindenbaum, Creator of the Sacred Depths Coach & Facilitator Training

THE ART OF LEADING CIRCLE

"I love Tanya's approach to teaching sacred circle facilitation. She makes it simple, giving women the confidence to take action, step into their leadership, and start a circle — as well as be compensated for the effort it takes to hold space for real transformation."

~ LiYana Silver, Women's coach and author of *Feminine Genius: The Provocative Path to Waking Up and Turning On the Wisdom of Being a Woman*

"Tanya hooked me from the first page and inspired me with her wisdom, contagious passion, and strategy to create a business by leading circles. She's figured it out and generously sharing it with every woman who wants it. She makes it simple, giving women the confidence to take action on their dreams. She's made me a believer than any woman can lead circle, they just need to follow the roadmap outlined in The Art of Leading Circle."

~ Kavita Rani Arora, Esq., Founder of Epic Dream Academy

"Women everywhere are wanting to gather in circle to reconnect with our roots and remember the ancient way of circling. Tanya provides an easy, comprehensive guide for women who want to step into their leadership and start their own circle. The world will be a better place because of it."

~ Naia Leigh, founder of Boundless Method, Women's Transformational Guide

Table of Contents

Introduction 1
   Why Circle? 3
   How Did We Get Here? And Where Do We Go? 7
   1 Million Circles: The Sistership Circle Path 11
   The Rise of the Feminine Leader 15
   The How to Lead Circle Blueprint 19

About Sistership Circle 27

Part One: How to Lead Circle 37
   Chapter 1:   Set Your Intentions 39
   Chapter 2:   Form the Masculine Container 45
   Chapter 3:   Trust the Feminine Flow 57
   Chapter 4:   Activate the Bonding Hormone
                     as the Mother 63
   Chapter 5:   Integrate After Circle 69
   Chapter 6:   Hold Sacred Space as the Priestess 75
   Chapter 7:   Be the Example and Embody
                     Feminine Leadership 83
   Chapter 8:   Create Engagement Through
                     Your Creativity 99
   Chapter 9:   Follow the Flow as the Wise Woman 103
   Chapter 10: May the Circle be Open but Unbroken 113

THE ART OF LEADING CIRCLE

Part 2: How to Start and Fill Circles 117

    Chapter 11:   Clarify Your Why to Lead 119

    Chapter 12:   Envision Your Intention................................... 125

    Chapter 13:   Commit with a Declaration 131

    Chapter 14:   Fill Your Circle Through the Art of Manifestation and Sharing 135

    Chapter 15:   Prepare Your Sacred Space 141

    Chapter 16:   Getting Started FAQs 149

    Chapter 17:   Avoid These Common Limited Beliefs 159

    Chapter 18:   Overcome Overwhelmed and Get Unstuck 163

Part 3: Growing Your Circle 167

    Chapter 19:   Keep the Momentum Going 169

    Chapter 20:   Embrace Collaboration 175

    Chapter 21:   Avoid Burnout 183

    Chapter 22:   Stay Radiant as the Queen 189

    Chapter 23:   Understand Community Building 195

    Chapter 24:   Make Money with the Circle Business Model 201

    Chapter 25:   Play Your Edge 211

    Chapter 26:   Keep the Circle Healthy 217

    Chapter 27:   Go Deeper in Your Healing 225

    Chapter 28:   Honor the Cycle 231

    Chapter 29:   Reflect and Take Your Next Step 239

    Chapter 30:   Closing 243

Dedication

To my husband, Brent, the man behind the movement.
Thank you for seeing me and my vision the day we met.
Thank you for sitting in circle to truly understand what we do.
Thank you for dedicating your genius to bring the Sistership Circle platform to life.
Thank you for urging me to write this book.

Acknowledgments

Sistership Circle would have never happened if it wasn't for Stephanie Armstrong approaching me at an event in 2010, asking for a weekly circle.

Over the years, I've circled with so many women I can't even count or remember all their names. But I acknowledge each and every woman who has been in Sistership Circle, believing in the power and magic of circle.

I also want to express my gratitude for the women past, present and future who dedicate their time and energy on our leadership team.

Laura Swan for your wisdom, sisterhood and co-creation for the first How to Lead Circle program.

Peta Bastian for your passion, vision, depth and devotion.

Sharlene Belusevic for your nurturing love, powerful meditations and countless hours of support.

Rae Ireland for bringing your magic, play, creativity and voice.

Kerstin Weibull Lundberg for your co-creative spirit, vision and intuition.

Natasha Daubney for your enthusiasm, dedication, and reliability.

The Sacred Nine for holding me in my vision.

THE ART OF LEADING CIRCLE

Elayne, Saida and Lisa for witnessing me in the ups and downs of my leadership.

All the Mastery women who've made me a wiser, better teacher.

Thank you to my support team at home, helping me focus on my life work.

And most of all, thank you to my power partner in life and business, Brent. Without you, this would have just been a few circles in San Diego. Your masculine support is invaluable. I honor you.

Introduction

"The circles of women around us weave invisible nets of love that carry us when we're weak and sing with us when we're strong."
~ SARK

Why Circle?

I'm Tanya Lynn, founder of Sistership Circle, author of *Open Your Heart: How to Be a New Generation Feminine Leader*, instructor for the Art of Leading Circle video course, and now author of *Art of Leading Circle*.

I have been leading events, workshops, retreats and circles for over a decade now, and have trained hundreds of women how to lead circle.

When I led my first circle, I had no idea what I was doing. It just kind of happened: a woman asked me to create a group of women to meet together weekly, and I created a circle for 12 women to meet for 12 weeks. I had no idea how complicated it would be. It felt messy. I felt incompetent. I didn't have a step by step blueprint to follow. So I took the long way around. And I kept going.

With each circle, more things came up. New challenges surfaced. And yet... *I just wanted more*. It felt like an unquenchable thirst. The good news is, I made a lot of mistakes and learned what works and what doesn't work. As a result, I created a shortcut for you to use, a secret formula that outlines exactly what to do from start to finish so you feel confident instead of overwhelmed.

The simple truth is, we need more women's circles on this planet. If you're reading these words, you have raised your hand as a torchbearer in this movement, and I want to take a moment to say thank you and extend a heartfelt welcome. I know you are ready to gather women and lead them in circle and you want to make sure that you know what you are doing so they get value and come back for more. You want

THE ART OF LEADING CIRCLE

to have the clarity and confidence to put your circle out there and to make that happen as quickly as possible.

I did it the hard way, but leading circle doesn't have to be messy, complicated, or exhausting. You simply need a big heart full of passion, a desire for connection, and a soul calling. The pull towards leading circle is unexplainable for most women who get into this work; it simply comes from a mysterious knowing deep within. When you combine that calling with the tools in this book, you'll feel confident, capable, and excited to create, fill, and lead your circles.

I started doing this work because I was *starving* for connection with other women. I had always been a tomboy and high-achieving athlete, feeling more comfortable hanging with the guys. I moved to New York City a few years after college to "make it" in the financial sales industry, but instead felt more disconnected, isolated, and lost in the constant go-go-go hustle of the city.

When I moved back to my hometown of San Diego, I wanted a change. I wanted sisterhood. So I started going to women's empowerment events and sitting in circle and then started putting on my own women-centered events. By being in circle, I developed the deep meaningful relationships with women that I craved, but more importantly, I found *myself* through the process. I learned how to accept my feelings, be more vulnerable, and soften into my feminine power. Circle became my lifeline, giving me hope and purpose.

And I realized something important: every woman needs this. But how could I bring this circle of sisterhood to more women? And how would I duplicate myself, teaching other women how to create these experiences in circle for others who needed it? As I went through my own transformation to become a more embodied and powerful leader,

WHY CIRCLE?

I developed a business model to help other women step into their feminine leadership and not only start leading circles, but to make money doing so.

As a complement to the Art of Leading Circle video course, this book follows a similar outline and structure. If you're already familiar with leading circle, you may want to use the book as a resource, looking up what you need in a specific section or keeping it on hand when questions arise. If you're newer to leading circle, it may be helpful to read through the book in order, as the tools described and discussed within build on each other. And remember to go at your own pace and according to your own learning style: some women may want to read through quickly and then revisit certain sections, while other women may want to read one section at a time with lots of space to digest in between. Know that any way you engage with the book is fine; what matters is that you're here, committed, and ready to learn more about how to lead circle.

I'd like to invite you now to commit fully: to yourself, to this process, and to learning all you can about how you can best lead your circles. While I believe any woman can lead circle, it does require effort on your part to make it happen. Remember, like in any venture, you will have grand successes and small setbacks. The important thing is to keep going, because by following the call and leading circle, you are helping to bring the divine feminine back to women and the world.

This is why I am so passionate about this work and why I have dedicated my life to bringing the ancient art of circle back to the modern world: so that every woman has access to circles and the healing and friendship which comes with them.

How Did We Get Here? And Where Do We Go?

"A woman is the full circle. Within her is the power to create, nurture and transform."
~ Diane Mariechild

Centuries ago, it was common for women to come together in circle every day, to support one another in birth and during the menstrual cycle, to cook and sew together, to take care of one another's children, and to share stories of inspiration and triumph. Women thrived in that nurturing, connective environment where they could lean on their village sisters in times of trouble and dance with them in times of celebration. But, with the Industrial Revolution and technological progress over the last century, women lost touch with the ancient art of circling and forgot the power of the feminine.

Now, however, it's come full circle. We are remembering this foundational way of being with one another. Look at how humans naturally circle in modern life. We sit in a circle around campfires to share stories. We gather in a circle around the table for dinner with our families. We sit in a group of friends with wine and talk about life. Women find comfort in gathering and being together, often circling without realizing it. With Sistership Circle, we are simply extending this practice to create *intentional* circles that gather together for support, healing, and celebration. And yet, it's important to remember that not every woman has access to a supportive circle of family or friends, and

THE ART OF LEADING CIRCLE

misses out on the connection, honesty, healing, and celebration circle provides.

In fact, have you noticed the massive division in the world today? Energetically, it feels as though everywhere in the world is split into an "us versus them" mentality. The patriarchal system we currently live in is based on the concepts of individuality and independence. As a result, women have been taught since childhood that we need to prove ourselves worthy by claiming "I can do it myself" in order to find our place in the world. This emphasis on the self over the community leads to mistrusting one another and competing with each other. The current state of society is so fragmented and separated. We are not working together as a human race, and so we continue to see war, destruction of our beautiful planet, and rampant dis-ease.

And yet through it all, people are searching for... *something*, a spiritual center, to find meaning in their lives. People want a solution to their feelings of isolation, distrust, and competition that will enable them to feel more fulfilled, happy, and on purpose. And that is exactly what circle provides.

When women circle, we learn to trust ourselves and one another. We step into our sovereignty as individuals while also learning how to be part of a collective. This is what I call the holy trinity of the divine feminine rising: circle, sisterhood, and feminine leadership. And this is what Sistership Circle is here to model and teach. This new model creates peace amongst people and harmony with the Earth.

What women fail to recognize is the power we truly hold. The patriarchy wants to keep us separated in order to break down our power. We've seen it over the course of history: not giving women the power to vote, to own property, and even to gather. Women were burned at the stake

HOW DID WE GET HERE? AND WHERE DO WE GO?

and often pitted against each other. With all of this silencing, it's no wonder women temporarily forgot how to use their voices. But when we come together as a unified sisterhood, supporting and celebrating each other, collaborating and co-creating together, we reclaim our power. This is the shift we are waiting for. This is how we will change the world.

If what circle pioneer Dr. Shinoda Bolen said is true, that 1 million circles will create a tipping point, then there is a huge opportunity and an enormous need, because while there has been a rising up of divine feminine energy on the planet, not every woman is circling yet.

1 Million Circles: The Sistership Circle Path

Our team of facilitators and trainers at Sistership Circle are on a mission to collectively create that tipping point of 1 million circles on the planet. When enough women understand our individual and collective power, then we are able to shift society on all levels: economically, socially, politically, and practically.

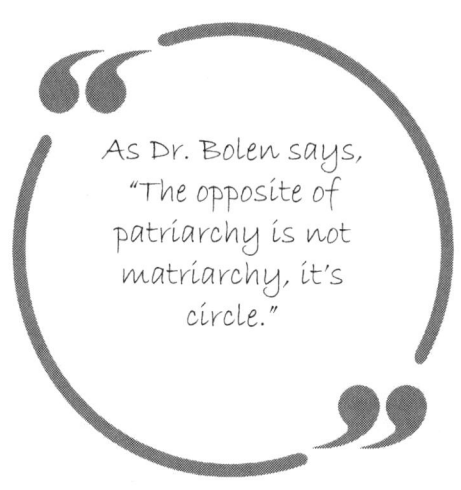

As Dr. Bolen says, "The opposite of patriarchy is not matriarchy, it's circle." Dr. Bolen's website is listed in the Resources section if you'd like to learn more about her. She is an expert in the archetypal psychology of men and women within the development of spirituality, and an influential leader whose rallying cry we have answered here at Sistership Circle. We don't want to replace men with women who do the same thing that is being done now, and thus perpetuating the patriarchy. We want to create a whole new model for the future, what we call "Co-Creative Leadership." We understand that we cannot do it on our own and neither can you. That's why you're here now.

THE ART OF LEADING CIRCLE

Co-Creative Leadership is like a wheel: each woman in circle is a spoke on the wheel, contributing her unique gifts, talents, strengths, and medicine, which is what makes the wheel turn. The wheel is created by the diversity of the community. Each woman contributes and together we co-create the mission, because we value and celebrate each woman's contribution and we are committed to her being her full self-expression. When we get that we each matter, that we each have something to offer, we can relax and stop trying to be everything to everyone. We can lean on our sisters and trust the law of giving and receiving. We'll be less exhausted and burned out in this new model. We'll learn how to collaborate and come together as one.

This new model starts in a circle of women and ripples out to their families, communities, and the world at large. We are here to create a unified movement, mission, platform, path, and community.

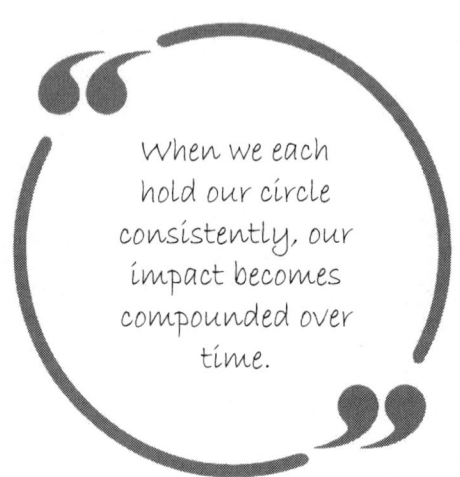

When we each hold our circle consistently, our impact becomes compounded over time.

I've trained hundreds of women to start their first circle and continue to hold circles month after month, year after year, because that momentum is exactly how this movement is going to spread: when we each hold our circle consistently, our impact becomes compounded over time.

It's my honor to pass the torch to you by teaching you the foundational structure for your circle to stand on its own two feet, as well as all my tips and tools to not only lead your circle but also to

1 MILLION CIRCLES: THE SISTERSHIP CIRCLE PATH

make women show up and keep coming back for more, to learn the subtle art of circle leadership.

Through this book and the Art of Leading Circle video course, I want to give you everything you need to lead a circle, whether it's a branded Sistership Circle or your own independent circle, because ultimately, there is no competition. The more circle facilitators there are around the world, the quicker we will get to that tipping point. I am also not going to deny the enormous opportunity to join forces with us, to be part of the Sistership Circle movement and be part of our community and use our platform. This does not mean you will have to fit into a mold that takes away your freedom, autonomy, or unique essence. You won't lose yourself; in fact, just the opposite happens.

We deliberately create spaciousness in our curriculums, giving each woman permission to make it her own. So, if you are someone who wants to contribute to a mission greater than yourself, because you don't want to do it all alone, and because you want to increase your impact and income with the Sistership Circle Business Model, you're invited to continue on the path by taking our level 1 certification course to become a licensed Sistership Circle Facilitator.

We have curriculums like no other organization out there to empower feminine leadership on the planet. We have a platform that functions as one central location, to lend you greater social proof, credibility, and exposure and to give you the tools and software you need to succeed. And we have a path to give you the necessary training to advance to the next level as a circle leader.

You can learn more about our path, and how to become part of Sistership Circle, at the end of the book.

THE ART OF LEADING CIRCLE

Just know that whatever path you choose, becoming a circle facilitator is one of the most powerful roles on the planet right now. Here at Sistership Circle, we predict that circle will become mainstream in the next decade. But not everyone wants to lead, so the circle facilitators of today are poised to make an incredible impact on the success of this movement.

The Rise of the Feminine Leader

> *"There is no force more powerful than*
> *a woman determined to rise."*
> *~ WEB Dubois*

We've been talking about how circle will change the world and why being a circle facilitator is one of the most exciting and rewarding roles in this "feminine rising" movement, but we need to define what we mean by the feminine and the concept of feminine leadership.

My favorite analogy for these concepts is "the feminine as a flower."

The first aspect of the feminine is who you are BEING. This can be represented by the petals of the flower. When the flower opens and reveals herself, sitting there glistening in the sun, not doing anything, the bees come to HER to drink her nectar. The feminine represents the wanting, enjoying, and feeling. When she is BEING in her essence, she is magnetic, radiant, and glowing.
When you soften and relax into your feminine, not trying to figure it out, you allow the circle to unfold like the petals of a flower opening.

The second aspect of the feminine, the core of the feminine, is within her DESIRE. I like to think of the desire as the nectar of the flower. This is what sparks that inspiration. This is what fills everyone up. This is what we call Awakening and Rising of the Feminine on this planet.

THE ART OF LEADING CIRCLE

When we say "feminine leadership," we are referring to women leading from these aspects of the feminine by applying feminine leadership principles to embody circle leadership.

There are three main principles that I want to share with you now:

1. **You are the example and act as a role model for others.** Feminine leadership is not limited to organizational, political, and corporate positions of power. Feminine leadership is about leading your own life, your family, and your community. You take full responsibility for your experience and walk your walk so that others feel empowered to follow your lead.

2. **You lead from your feminine superpowers.** Feminine leadership draws on your strengths as a woman-- your intuition, creativity, and ability to feel and connect-- while simultaneously integrating the divine masculine so that you are an embodied woman, whole and complete within yourself.

3. **You co-create and collaborate with others.** You cannot be a feminine leader operating as a solo individual. That's old patriarchal model. You need to embrace sisterhood. Feminine leadership is focused on WE, us, the collective, which requires you to dismantle your ego, heal the divide you experience with other women, and know that you are more powerful when you link arms with other women instead of trying to do it all by yourself. This requires you to develop your ability to give *and* receive.

Feminine leadership is crucial, because if you think back to the witch-burning days, women were pitted against each other, and from generation to generation, women have passed on that hurt, betrayal,

THE RISE OF THE FEMININE LEADER

jealousy, competition, comparison, and mistrust. This generational hurt is what we call the Sister Wound. It's prevalent in our culture and epitomized by movies and TV shows displaying women competing against and betraying each other.

Thankfully, it's in circle where we learn how to honor, celebrate, and support one another and to open our hearts to one another instead of gossiping behind each other's backs, backstabbing and stealing from one another, and competing against and comparing ourselves to one another.

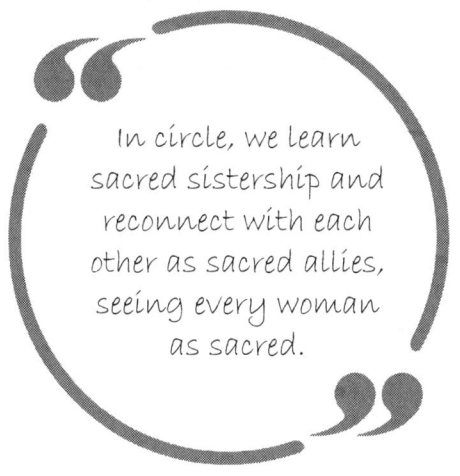

In circle, we learn sacred sistership and reconnect with each other as sacred allies, seeing every woman as sacred.

In circle, we learn sacred sistership and reconnect with each other as sacred allies, seeing every woman as sacred. This is the holy trinity of Circle, Sisterhood, and Feminine Leadership: these three go hand in hand. They cannot exist without each other.

And as a circle leader, 90% of your job is to embody the holy trinity. Just 10% is the skill set of facilitation: the tools, techniques and structural elements. Our philosophy here at Sistership Circle is built on the foundation of these distinctions of feminine leadership.

We also focus on transformational facilitation. According to the Oxford dictionary, transformation is defined as "a thorough or dramatic change in form or appearance." The circle leadership we are talking about here is different from leading a support group or book club. The circles we teach you to lead are spaces where women enter and

THE ART OF LEADING CIRCLE

become a completely different person, the woman they want to be, by the time they leave. This kind of transformational facilitation is focused on growth, healing, and empowerment. There are three key distinctions to remember as we move forward:

1. **We have an integrated Masculine and Feminine Approach to circle.** This is the container and the energy inside the container. We need structure, curriculum, and boundaries for the feminine magic to occur inside of us.

2. **We believe anyone can lead circle**. The key to circle working is when the facilitator is herself. She's not trying to be a guru; she's authentic, real, and vulnerable.

3. **We teach the KISS format**. Keep it simple, sweetheart. Transformation occurs when we simplify and create space for the magic of circle to "work on" the participants.

The How to Lead Circle Blueprint

The concepts of feminine leadership and transformational facilitation essentially describe who you need to be to lead engaging circle experiences that impact women's lives. I shared with you that the embodiment, or who you are being, is 90% of the work, and the other 10% is the skill sets and tools. Now we're going to go into the "how to" of actually building and leading a circle-- but before we do that, I need to disclose a common pitfall.

Women get so caught up on the "how to" lead circle and think that a circle outline is going to be the answer to all their prayers.

It's not.

The blueprint I am about to share with you gives you the bigger picture, filling in the gaps that are missing before and after the circle outline. But the blueprint is worthless if you are stuck in your fears. From my experience and training other women to lead circle, there are four main fears that come up, each associated with limited beliefs that sabotage women's efforts to actually lead circle. Let's break these fears down.

Fear 1: The fear of putting it out there.
    Limiting Beliefs: You're too weird. You're too woo-woo. You're too much. It's not safe to be your true self.

Fear 2: The fear of women not showing up.
    Limiting Beliefs: You're not popular enough. You don't know enough people. *You're* not enough. You will be rejected.

THE ART OF LEADING CIRCLE

Fear 3: The fear of women showing up… and you disappointing them.
Limiting Beliefs: You are incapable. You are a fraud.

Fear 4: The fear of putting in all this effort-- and they don't come back.
Limiting Beliefs: You didn't create enough transformation. You can't make a difference.

You didn't do enough.

But here's the thing: The fears that stem from these limiting beliefs *are not who you are.*

I want to share a powerful mantra that I use to help me shift my mindset:

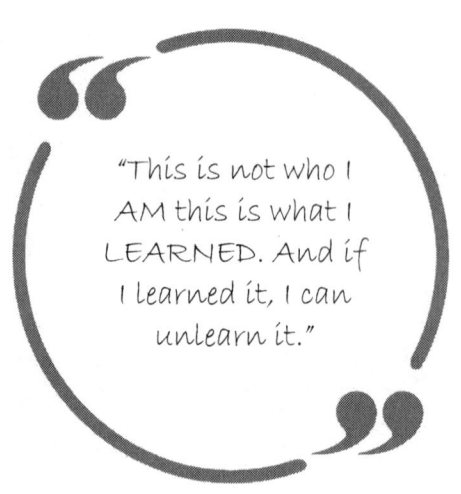

"This is not who I AM this is what I LEARNED. And if I learned it, I can unlearn it."

"This is not who I AM this is what I LEARNED. And if I learned it, I can unlearn it."

While you are experiencing a fear, that fear is not your truth. The truth is who you *are*, not what you learned. When you tap into your truth and remember who you are, you become unstoppable. When you tap into your truth, you come to realize that you are worthy and deserving of having your desires, and that you are worthy of not only leading circle, but also getting paid for it.

20

THE HOW TO LEAD CIRCLE BLUEPRINT

Now let's reframe these beliefs.

Place one your hand on your heart and one hand on your womb and repeat after me:

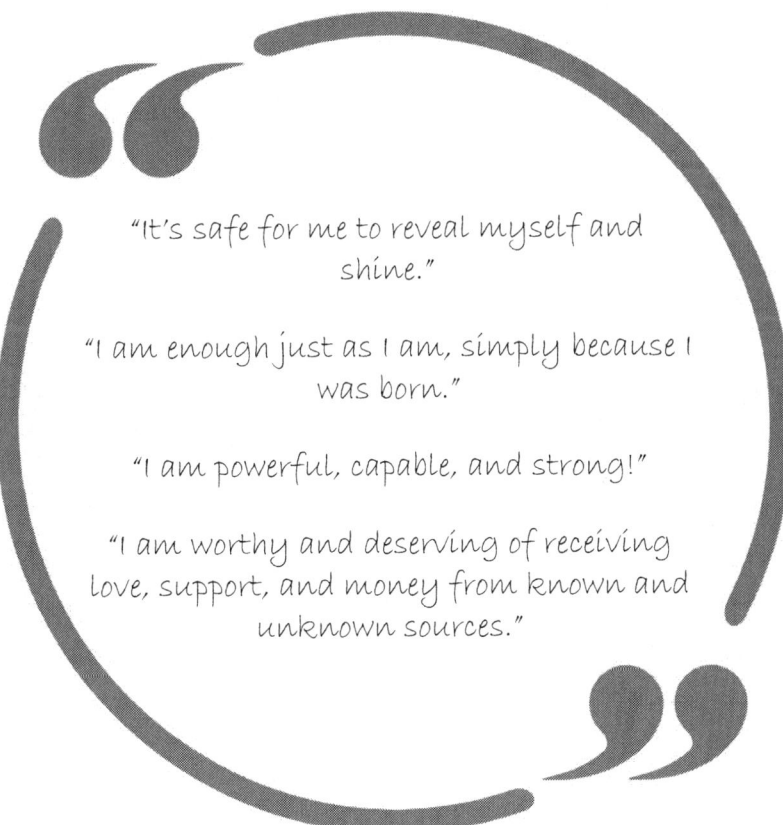

"It's safe for me to reveal myself and shine."

"I am enough just as I am, simply because I was born."

"I am powerful, capable, and strong!"

"I am worthy and deserving of receiving love, support, and money from known and unknown sources."

Now I want to give you the solution to help you embody these power statements through action with the 9 pillars of the How to Lead Circle Blueprint, or the 9 C's of Circle.

21

THE ART OF LEADING CIRCLE

This is about you creating a highly engaged, transformational circle that you can get paid for, no matter how much prior experience you have. So, if you are just starting out, this will help you feel confident to create a circle you can charge money for in the next 90 days. And if you are already leading circles, this will help you expand your circles and your offerings with a more comprehensive business model.

The How to Lead Circle Blueprint is focused on how to *fill*, *lead*, and *grow* your circles and create something that women show up for, not just once, but again and again.

Let's start with how to *fill* your circles:

Pillar 1: Clarity

When you know your desire, you become clearer in your intention and therefore create a clear opening for women to come in. This clarity from the feminine is magnetic. We'll take you through a process to clarify your desire, or your why, in Chapter 11.

Pillar 2: Confidence

Your confidence is trusting the voice of your own inner authority. Your confidence comes when you really *get* that you have all the answers within you. Your confidence comes when you know who you are, the value of the unique gifts that you bring, and the power that you hold. You discover this truth when you sit in circle and have other women reflect back to you what they see: your light, your unique essence, your power, your strengths. Circle is the place where we start to feel safe to reveal our true selves. When we find the courage to speak up in circle, we then feel confident to put ourselves out there in the world.

THE HOW TO LEAD CIRCLE BLUEPRINT

We'll cover many tools in Section 2 to build your confidence as a circle leader.

Pillar 3: Collaboration

Remember when I talked about letting go of doing it on your own? Well, one of the most powerful tools you can use to fill your circles is collaborating with other women. This is how I built Sistership Circle-- not alone, but in collaboration.

In Chapter 20, I'll teach you the 4 steps you need to take to bring on collaboration partners so they can support your circle business.

The next pillars cover how to *lead* your circles.

Pillar 4: Connection

Women come to circle for connection. And in order for women to connect, they must be given permission to open up and get real. To create that space for connection, it's important that you model authenticity and vulnerability. All you need to do is show up as yourself.

We'll go over some of the ways you can create an immediate connection (even amongst strangers!) in Chapter 3.

Pillar 5: Container

The container is the masculine structure that serves and supports the *why*, or the feminine. There are specific elements that will help you create that container with integrity.

THE ART OF LEADING CIRCLE

Pillar 6: Co-Creation.

If you were leading a workshop, the focus would be on you teaching everything by yourself to the group. But leading circle is different in that the focus is on the connection, which is what makes it so appealing because you don't need to know anything to get started. To take this principle a step further, when you bring co-creation into your circles, you create even more powerful experiences. There are 7 ways to have the women in your circle take ownership which you'll learn about in Chapter 7, so you aren't doing it all yourself, which ultimately creates more engagement and ease within your circle.

And finally, let's cover the pillars for how to *grow* your circles.

Pillar 7: Currency.

We cannot have this conversation about circles without talking about money in Chapter 24. There is a stigma around money: that circles should be free, that sisterhood cannot be commoditized, and that it's not "spiritual" or "healing" if you're charging money. These stigmas need to be broken down so that circle can be an equitable vehicle for the rise of the divine feminine for women everywhere.

Pillar 8: Commitment.

To build and grow your circles into a business, you must commit yourself *and* have the women in your circles make a deeper commitment. We'll talk about the circle business model and how the second stage requires commitment to increase your income as a circle leader.

Pillar 9: Community.

Without building a community that is bigger than you, you can't really grow your circles. All of the pillars that we have mentioned so far create a real community of women who have each other's backs and support one another's dreams, a community that is rooted in love and dedicated to sacred sistership and feminine leadership.

We're going to cover how to build this type of community in Chapter 23.

About Sistership Circle

Before we go any further, I want you to understand what Sistership Circle really is and what we do, so that you have context for what you're learning and how it applies to the larger world around you.

Sistership Circle began in 2009 when I led my very first circle. I'd moved home to San Diego after living in New York City and working in the financial industry. I felt disconnected, isolated, and lonely in New York and wanted to start over in closer proximity to my family. While in New York, I went to Landmark Education and the Institute for Integrative Nutrition, starting my lifelong journey of personal development and growth. I also longed for sisterhood and the feeling of community that I learned as a child living on a 2 acre property with my family where we often hosted gatherings of 50 people or more.

I thought if I wanted it, then I needed to build it. I put on my first event, called "Women for Wellness," in 2009 to bring like-minded women together to talk about healthy living. That event was so popular that I continued to host monthly gatherings, which evolved into Tribal Truth in 2010, when I partnered with a woman and we started to spread our events to different cities.

Over time, however, things no longer felt quite on the mark. I wanted more and fell out of alignment with my business partner. And to make it worse, my boyfriend who I was living with at the time broke up with me. I tried to hold it together but ended up crying on a call with some of my team members. One of the women on that call said to me, "Wow, Tanya I feel so connected to you! Like you are a real human!" I

THE ART OF LEADING CIRCLE

had always thought I needed to constantly be strong and put together to lead. But what I discovered is that in order to create those deeper connections, I had to be vulnerable and authentic.

> *Leadership is not pretending to have your life perfectly together, leadership is being vulnerable enough to be messy so that other women have permission to let go of the "good girl" act and just be real.*

Everything changed that day. That was the beginning of my unraveling and learning how to lead from an embodied, integrated place. The more I leaned into circle, the more I fell apart. The little girl who wanted to make her father proud by succeeding in the world finally got to feel all the emotions she'd bottled up and stored away. The women in my circles held me while I sobbed and screamed. I learned that leadership is not pretending to have your life perfectly together, leadership is being vulnerable enough to be messy so that other women have permission to let go of the "good girl" act and just be real. By finally letting go of the false sense of self, I found my true, integrated self. I am both fierce and soft. I am both a purpose-driven entrepreneur and a loving, present mother. I have learned to play my full range of emotions through circle and live in full self-expression.

Leading circle has been my vehicle for healing, self-growth, and leadership development. It has made me into an incredible mother, wife, business owner, sister, friend, and daughter. It has supported me emotionally, spiritually, energetically, financially, and physically. Women

ABOUT SISTERSHIP CIRCLE

from circle have even shown up to take care of my household after I gave birth and held me when I lost my second baby in a miscarriage.

I started to train other women how to lead circle from a place of authenticity and held the container for other women to heal, transform, and celebrate sisterhood. And in 2014, after meeting my husband Brent, we officially launched Sistership Circle to put in the systems and structures to grow this organization globally. Brent and I work together with a beautiful balance of the masculine and feminine, which has translated to a better, more balanced business.

I am so passionate about teaching women how to lead circle and how to scale it so they can feel fulfilled in their life purpose while also having their own safe haven to be supported. Circle is for me just as much as it is for the other women in it.

Sistership Circle is not only an organization but also a movement with a vision and mission. Our mission is to give every woman in the world the experience of real and authentic sistership where she is loved, accepted, and celebrated as herself.

Feel that for a minute.

What if every single woman in the world felt loved, accepted, and celebrated?

What would that type of healing do for the planet?

We believe that through sistership, women gain confidence in being a woman, claim their feminine leadership, and develop meaningful, deep connections with other women. It's about being sovereign individuals coming together in deep, meaningful relationships with one another.

THE ART OF LEADING CIRCLE

The rise of women, in sistership, standing shoulder to shoulder in solidarity, reclaiming our individual and collective power. That unity which comes from all waving the same flag, that power of all being under the same umbrella, instead of fragmented and isolated silos not on the same page, not supporting each other, and not working toward a common goal.

I'm reminded of the story of Leymah Gbowee, one of my all-time favorite heroines, who won the Nobel Peace Prize and wrote the book *Mighty Be Our Powers*. Leymah rallied women to come together in circle to protest the war in Siberia. It was through sisterhood that they stopped the war and made history.

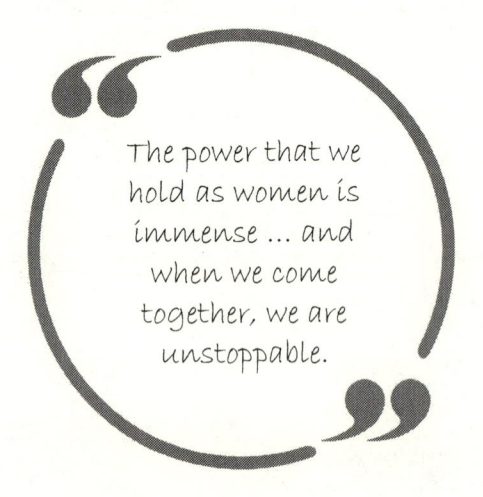

> The power that we hold as women is immense ... and when we come together, we are unstoppable.

Here is our vision at Sistership Circle:

Our vision is seeing a world with more than one million circles being led, where "circle" is woven into the fabric of society, and every woman has access to a circle. Where the world shifts from patriarchy to equality and feminine leadership is encouraged and celebrated. Where women rise together and support one another.

ABOUT SISTERSHIP CIRCLE

Our vision is seeing a world where women create safety for themselves and each other and all strive to be BRAVE: bold, responsible, authentic, vulnerable, and empathetic.

Our vision is seeing a world where women are committed to healing the sister wound and where the next generations of women and girls love themselves, speak their truth, and know their worth.

Our mission and vision may sound impossible, but it's the impossible missions that are worth fighting for.

So, how do we make this vision a reality?

At Sistership Circle, we believe it's by creating a path for women to rise together.

One mission.
So we can put our collective energy and intention on achieving it together. It keeps us laser-focused and motivated to contribute to something greater than ourselves.

One platform.
So we bring more social proof and brand equity, which compounds over time as more women come on board. This is critical to building momentum and bringing this concept mainstream, as we are all directing people to a common place to see the work we are doing together.

One path.
So we can understand what each other is going through as we use the same curriculums and focus on achieving the next level of growth. This provides accountability and support to increase our impact, income, and influence both as individuals and as a collective.

THE ART OF LEADING CIRCLE

Now, I want to take a moment to tell you about our certification program.

Reading this book is a great first step to learning about leading and growing a circle. But it's simply not enough for most women to feel completely ready and supported to BE a circle facilitator. It does not give you the full certification as a Sistership Circle Facilitator, or afford you the advantages of our branding, resources, and platform.

The Sistership Circle certification training goes much more in-depth into our process and the bar we set as an organization. We want any woman, anywhere in the world, to be able to go to a Sistership Circle and know that they are going to be held in a container that is safe and proven. That is what the certification training does.

Don't get me wrong, this book is *exactly* the right first step! You're going to be ready to lead your first circle and promote it, and that is AWESOME.

But what we have seen time and again is that many women start on their own, and end up leading one, two, or five circles, and then fizzle out. It still feels like a singular, isolated process to them. It's like making a New Years Resolution: the initial rush feels great! You commit to doing it often, and then... after a while, you start doing it less and less and lose motivation and life obligations get in the way.

So, we've developed our certification path to provide accountability, support, and hands-on training. You'll have support when you need it, answers to all your questions, help when you face a new obstacle or challenge, and you'll also get to take advantage of the Sistership Circle branding, access to our circle outlines, free marketing material, and use of our website and platform. Instead of feeling like you're doing it

ABOUT SISTERSHIP CIRCLE

alone, you get the value and credibility of a global brand behind you and the help, support, and resources you need to increase your impact and make supplemental income as a Sistership Circle Facilitator.

There are four levels to the Sistership Circle certification path. Each level is designed to help women rise up to their next level of leadership. You must complete the level 1 program to gain access to all of our tools, platform, and resources.

As a Level 1 Sistership Circle facilitator, you're laser-focused on impacting as many women as possible through monthly gatherings and creating authentic connections. To achieve level 1, you will complete the How to Lead Circle Program, a 12-week course where you'll participate and co-lead circles while learning the Sistership Circle methodologies. In the Level 1 training, you are surrounded by support and accountability and learn how to establish a community. At this point, you are holding monthly gatherings with the intention of building your community and gathering enough women and interest to fill your first 12-week experience. You're provided with all the necessary tools, support, accountability, and fresh content to have women coming back for more month after month.

Level 2 of our certification program is called the Business of Circle, an intensive 4-month program designed to up-level your leadership and teach you how to launch our proven 8-week circle program. Monthly circle gatherings are wonderful, but you can go even deeper and create more transformation with an 8 or 12-week program in your community, not to mention also increasing your income. Level 2 is all about embodying feminine leadership. There is more flow and ease as you are implementing the Sistership Circle system, and you believe in our mission in every cell of your body.

THE ART OF LEADING CIRCLE

As a Level 2 Sistership Circle facilitator, you have established yourself as a leader in your community and are consistently drawing women to the movement. You are present to the difference you're making through circle and the transformation occurring in the women in your circle programs, which is making you feel even more confident in your leadership.

To achieve Level 3 certification, you complete our 9-month journey called Mastery of Circle and step in your next level of visibility as a pillar in the Sistership Circle movement, leading the feminine uprising on the planet by facilitating at our Feminine Uprising Live event. In Mastery of Circle, you'll learn to integrate coaching into your repertoire and lead your community on retreats and additional transformative workshops.

As a Level 3 Sistership Circle facilitator, you've mastered the art of circle and have woven it into your everyday life, so your life feels like a ceremony. You've masterfully integrated circles with coaching so you can work with women at many different levels. You've established yourself as a pillar in the circle movement and women look to you for leadership and inspiration to guide the movement forward. You are an empowered and embodied facilitator.

As a Level 4 Sistership Circle facilitator, you've demonstrated your leadership and your natural next step is to train other facilitators. You've successfully completed our Train the Trainer program and have joined the Sistership Circle training team to ignite the leadership in women joining the movement. You are implementing the Sistership Circle Business Model with monthly gatherings, longer circle programs, coaching, workshops, and retreats, and are now able to teach and coach others to do the same from an embodied experience.

ABOUT SISTERSHIP CIRCLE

If you feel inspired by what we are co-creating and you want to be part of something greater than yourself while getting all of the support, accountability, and mentorship you need to rise up in your leadership, your next step would be joining the 12-week How to Lead Circle Program and achieving your Level 1 certification with Sistership Circle.

We'll even give you everything you need to market and host a circle in your town to be part of our worldwide Sistership Circle Day, where we have hundreds of circles happening simultaneously all over the world.

Imagine the load taken off your shoulders with a platform that gives you everything you need: circle outlines, marketing materials, a page to display your events. You'll be part of our map, alongside so many other circle leaders all over the world. Imagine the credibility and social proof this brand can give you.

As an important note, I don't want you to feel that this book you are currently reading is not valuable and useful. But women who start out on their own feel isolated and want to contribute to a movement greater than themselves. They also find that they need additional accountability to really launch their own circle business and come into their own as a facilitator, which is why we developed our certification course, to further your studies and give you additional support and resources.

You can be part of something huge at Sistership Circle and help fulfill our collective mission and vision of 1 million circles. There's a reason you came here. And we'd love to welcome you aboard if you feel the call.

Now, let's get into how to lead circle!

DEAR SISTER

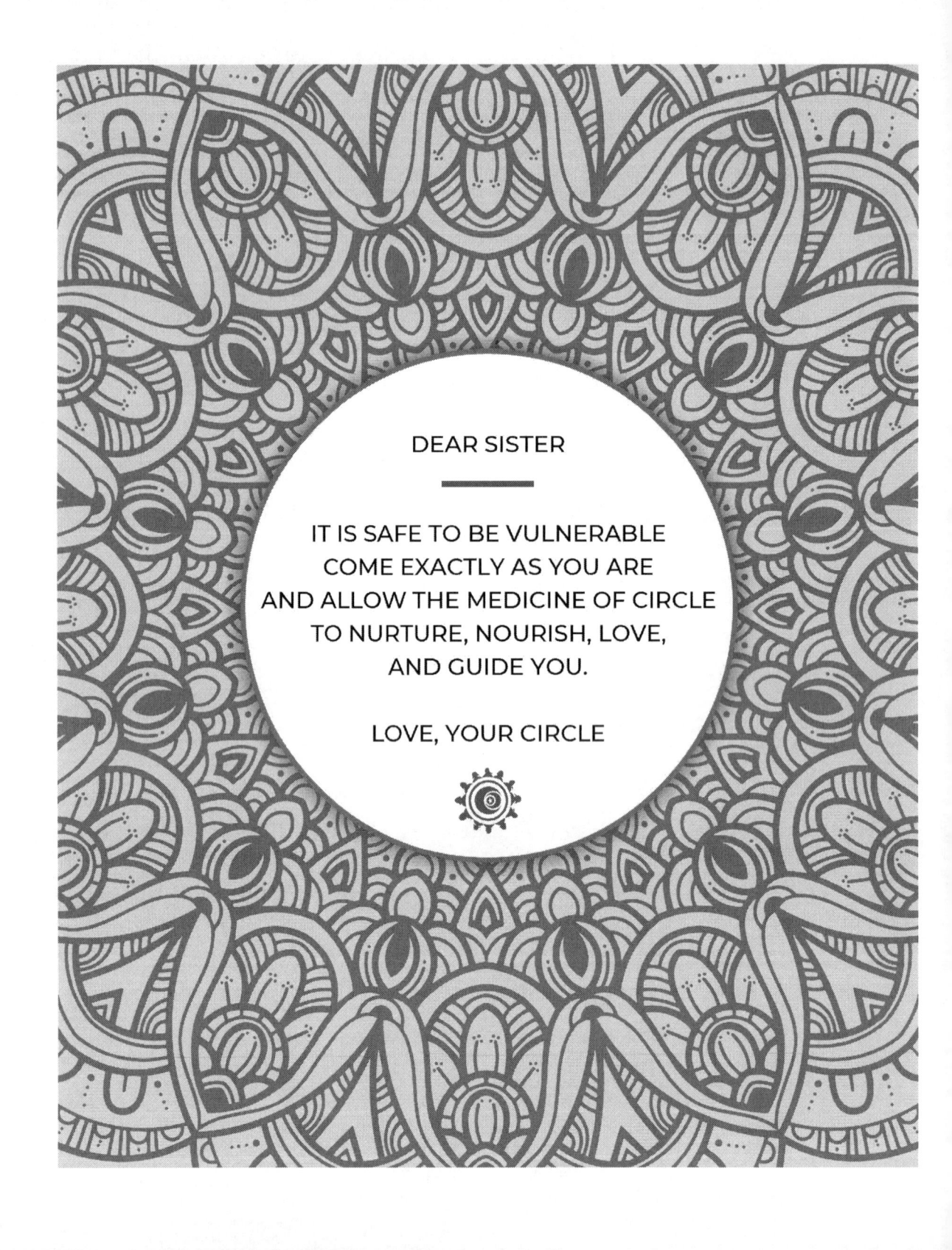

IT IS SAFE TO BE VULNERABLE
COME EXACTLY AS YOU ARE
AND ALLOW THE MEDICINE OF CIRCLE
TO NURTURE, NOURISH, LOVE,
AND GUIDE YOU.

LOVE, YOUR CIRCLE

Part One: How to Lead Circle

We're going to dive into how to lead your circles by covering all the facilitation tools needed to create a powerful experience. We start with the fundamentals of facilitating circles, which will give you the tools you need to be a fantastic circle leader. As I mentioned in the introduction, I believe anyone can lead circle. Leading circle is not reserved for "gurus," therapists, or specialists. It does not require any specialized knowledge. You do not need to teach anything. In fact, I highly discourage trying to be a guru in circle, because then you are countering the whole idea of circling in the first place.

To lead circle, you need to first learn the basic elements of circle, so that you can hold the container as the facilitator and then be and believe in yourself in order to help other women do the same.

I believe that by understanding the structure of the circle and what you are providing, you will feel more confident to go out there and tell women to come experience it with you. We're going to go step by step through how to set up your circle, giving you both the energetic and structural elements so that you understand what it means to be a circle facilitator.

Here are just some of the things we'll cover in Part One:

- The things you must know before, during and after your circle
- How to create immediate connection amongst women, even if they are strangers

THE ART OF LEADING CIRCLE

- How to hold space effectively so women can show up and be real

- The value of being the example and three ways to embody feminine leadership

- When to use your intuition and go away from your circle outline

- The elements of a circle outline and how to use your creativity to make your own content

- The listening tool you want to use to create more flow in your circles

Set Your Intentions

"Intentions are like magnets; the more we declare them, believe in them, and act in ways to manifest them, the more powerful and real they become."
~ Unknown

When women come to your circle, you want them to feel like they are coming to a safe and sacred space, right? Of course you do, and you are reading this book because you want to know how to create that space.

The key is this: it's all about the container you hold. The circle container consists of both the masculine structure and the feminine flow, or the magical energy that brings it alive.

For example, if you have a glass of water, you can think of the glass as the masculine structure and the water as the feminine flow. The water can slosh around, but it stays contained and safe and doesn't spill

THE ART OF LEADING CIRCLE

> *For us to cultivate really strong, potent energy in a circle, we need to build a strong container to hold that energy.*

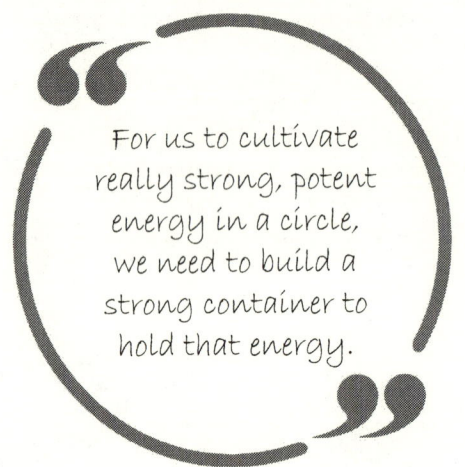

all over the place. This example illustrates that what we're talking about is a way of containing energy. If the water spills out, what happens to the water? It seeps into the ground and is no longer there. For us to cultivate really strong, potent energy in a circle, we need to build a strong container to hold that energy.

The first step is to set up your container with an intention. I cannot stress this part enough; it is the most important energetic part of circle.

Our thoughts become our words become our actions. Reality, the outer world, is simply a manifestation of the inner landscape of our minds. This is why intentions are so powerful. When we put our attention *on* our intentions, they become our reality. Before stepping into circle, you must set some intentions for yourself, for the women in the circle, and for the space you are holding. The intention for the circle is the foundation that provides everything you need to create a context for the circle. Intention gives direction and allows for the circle to do its magic. Intention allows you to let go and trust in a higher power. Intentions are about a way of BEING.

I set a two-fold intention for each time the women gather in circle.

1. My personal intention for myself: what I want to receive.

2. An intention for the group: what I want us all to walk away with at the end of circle.

SET YOUR INTENTIONS

Before circle, write the intentions on the top of your notes for your agenda or timeline. This will make sure you can quickly reference them and stay on track. You can read this intention to the group at the beginning of the circle, or you can keep the intention to yourself. It doesn't matter, because the intention is energetic, which means it's in the collective unconscious of the circle either way.

Have the women also set their own individual intentions at the start of the program each time they meet. This can be done either silently in meditation or by sharing in front of a partner or the entire group. Remember, circle is a mirror. Whatever happens in circle, happens in life. Whatever I am feeling, someone else in the circle is also feeling. By setting intentions individually and sharing them collectively, we see our common purpose.

When we have an intention, we then trust that we will get exactly what we need in circle. I refer to this as the "circle medicine." The circle is the space for our intentions to be realized. When we want something, sometimes we have to overcome obstacles. The circle may provide some mirrors that are not so nice to look at. This is the shadow side of circle, what makes it real and authentic. It's not all rainbows and butterflies. Like life, there is day and night, darkness and light, winter and summer, illness and health. The medicine, the circle itself, helps us heal the parts of ourselves we have shamed or deemed to be "bad" and "wrong." The circle medicine aids the transformation to occur.

The intention setting process is truly crucial to create a valuable transformational circle experience.

Once you have your intention, the next step is to create a structure to hold that intention. In the next chapter, we'll go over in detail the

THE ART OF LEADING CIRCLE

structure of a circle, so you have the tools to support yourself and the women in your circle within this divine container.

Featured Facilitator: Peta Bastian

Despite being drenched with jet lag and walking around in a daze collecting my luggage following a 26-hour flight from Australia, I could hardly contain my excitement as I landed in San Diego last year. Not only was I minutes away from seeing one of my best friends after five years, but I was also about to co-lead a five-day retreat with a group of Sistership Circle Mastery of Circle students whose lives I had been blessed to be a part of as they followed their dream of being a circle facilitator journeying through the facilitator pathway… just as I had five years prior.

Pulling into an abrupt stop at the passenger pickup was a golden SUV. The driver's door flung open and out jumped a screaming Tanya running toward me with her arms in the air. I ran screaming as well and we hugged and jumped up and down like schoolgirls, bags strewn across the road - we literally stopped traffic. What a reunion!!

When I first began leading circles, one of my main intentions was to heal the sisterhood wound; I longed for deep, connected friendships I could trust, and yet I was scared of getting close because honestly, women scared me. Leading circles was the exact medicine I needed and as I've grown my facilitation skills to a level of mastery, I know that by giving myself exactly what I need in circle I am able to create that space for others, too.

Over the years, the reasons why I lead and train other women to be circle facilitators has evolved as I have evolved. But one thing has never changed: Before every circle I create an intention that is real, alive, and relevant for me at that moment by simply closing my eyes, going within through the breath, with one hand on my heart. I ask myself "How do I want to FEEL?" and then I sit and listen. Listen to my body, listen to my heart, and allow myself to open up to what I want to receive… if I'm

SET YOUR INTENTIONS

tired, then I want to feel loved and supported. If I'm excited, then I want to feel playful. If I'm sluggish, then I want to feel invigorated. If I'm disconnected, then I want to feel heard... Whatever comes to me first is perfect and I trust it completely.

Why do I set the intention for myself first before the other women in circle? Because you can't give from an empty cup. Unless you feel fully resourced, you will not be able to extend your capacity to hold space for others.

Now comes the really magical part... Now you get to tune in to the intention you wish to set for the circle and the women who come.

At the beginning of our Mastery Retreat, Tanya and I each created a word to represent our intention for the upcoming retreat. Next, we created the intention for the students, which was for each of them to have a breakthrough that would deepen their leadership skills, and we distilled it down into one word for each woman. We then painted the words onto large beach pebbles ready to gift to the women at the completion of our retreat. In our final circle, each woman shared her reflection of the retreat and what she had received, Tanya and I sat in amazement, pinching each other as almost every woman SAID THE EXACT WORD that we had painted on the pebble for them. BOOM! That is the power of intention and that is the magic of circle.

Form the Masculine Container

"Boundaries are basically about providing structure, and structure is essential in building anything that thrives."
~ Henry Cloud

I have found that structure is essential to having effective circles. I think a lot of women avoid and dislike structure because they believe that they and their circles should be immersed completely in this feminine flow. But the truth is, having a structure in place is what allows the flow to occur. If you don't have structure, your circle can easily fall apart. As a facilitator, you want to make sure that you have a rough structural outline and the various elements to create safety so that you can actually create that flow you desire.

The following elements describe the structure of circle from start to finish.

THE ART OF LEADING CIRCLE

Element 1: The Opening Ceremony

Women have entered the space, and you're now ready to sit down and start circle. The first thing that you want to do is make sure that you have a strong opening.

Help the women ground their energy by starting with a meditation. This meditation should help women arrive in their space within the circle, to let go of their day so they can be fully present, and to drop out of their head and into their body. After the meditation, once the women are grounded and present in their bodies, we create safety.

> Women feel safe when they feel connected.

Women feel safe when they feel connected. So, how can you create immediate connection at your circle, even or maybe especially when it is a bunch of strangers? At Sistership Circle we have a special ritual in the opening ceremony called "The Stitch," where everyone shares their name and intention, and then I have everyone go around and give each other hugs. Hug time is my secret to immediate connection.

You'll notice that when you prioritize hug time at the beginning of circle, the energy of the room goes up about twenty notches. Women become alive. They let down their guard. They are ready to now share their hearts with one another, because they feel connected. It's pure magic.

FORM THE MASCULINE CONTAINER

Element 2: The Agreements

Once the women in your circle feel connected to each other, they can more easily and authentically agree to the necessary agreements of being in circle together. The three most basic agreements that you want to make sure that you put in place at the start of circle are confidentiality, timing, and feedback.

I like to use the word *agreements* instead of *rules* because *rules* sounds kind of like a dictator ("You have to do this!") while agreements are co-creative. Agreements allow everyone to be on the same page. It's how we relate to the container and to one another.

It's important to understand how these agreements benefit the container and the women within circle. Agreements continue to create that necessary safety within the circle space and allow women to be fully present in their experiences.

The first agreement, **confidentiality**, makes sure that everyone feels safe to be able to share whatever's on their heart. Have your entire circle agree, out loud, that this circle is a confidential space and no one will share anyone's story, message, or trauma with any person outside of the group. Whatever is said in the circle stays in the circle, so women can allow themselves to be vulnerable, honest, and open with themselves and with each other.

The second agreement, **timing**, maintains the integrity that is essential to a safe container. This agreement has two parts.

First is the timing of the circle itself. If you say the circle ends at 9:00 p.m., make sure that you end at 9:00 p.m. If you're going to go a little bit over, let people know that you're going to go a little bit over,

THE ART OF LEADING CIRCLE

and give them permission to leave if they need to. Ideally, however, try to stay within your timeframe. People have other obligations and commitments, and you want to honor them.

The other agreement around timing is with sharing. If you're going to have sharing, the last thing that you want is for people to go past their time limit, so that the last woman has no time left to share. Having a physical timer is a great way for you as the circle leader to not have to feel like you are policing the circle yourself, since the timer can do that job for you. Explain about the timer at the beginning of sharing time and let everyone know that when the timer goes off, it's time to wrap up their share so that everyone gets equal time to share.

The final agreement is around **feedback**. If a woman in the circle has some kind of emotional breakdown, or if someone starts crying, do you want the rest of the women to jump in to fix, coach and rescue one another? The answer is no.

Circle is about honoring each woman's experience. We have a saying at Sistership Circle: "issue with the tissues," and have created an agreement around not offering a tissue when someone is crying. Although you may think that you're being compassionate, when you pass a woman a tissue or try to console her, you cut off her experience. Paying attention to the "tissue" actually brings her out of the emotion she's experiencing and back into her head.

The agreement here is no feedback, which includes advice giving, fixing, coaching, rescuing, and consoling. By eliminating feedback, each woman really gets to be in the experience of finding the answers within herself and not looking for external validation. Through this process, you will notice women start to trust themselves more and speak

FORM THE MASCULINE CONTAINER

their truth more confidently. This is one of the biggest transformations in circle.

Element 3: Create Context

The next thing that you want to do is create context by talking about what you are going to do. You do this by creating a circle outline. At the beginning of your circle, share a little bit about the theme and give them a rough overview of your outline.

Here's an example from one of the monthly circle outlines that we provide our Level 1 facilitators:

Our theme for today's circle is 'Activate Abundance,' and we will begin by taking a moment to contemplate this quote by Marianne Williamson:

"If you dwell within abundance you will have abundance."

Each of us has our own relationship with abundance. It often starts at a young age as we develop our abundance blueprint based on our experiences as a child.

Many of us have had experiences in childhood where all our needs were not provided for by our mothers. And so the result is that we have disconnected from Mother Earth and from the Divine Mother. We no longer trust that she is really there for us and that all our needs will be met.

In tonight's circle, we are going to reconnect with the Divine Mother with the intention to cultivate trust that our needs will be met, so we can open ourselves up to receive abundance from the universe. We'll start with a group share, then I'll guide you through a visualization, a ritual, some movement, and finally some more sharing before we close the circle by 9:30pm. How's that sound sisters?

THE ART OF LEADING CIRCLE

Element 4: The Group Share

The group share is where you ask everyone to go around and share their thoughts, feelings, or anything they want on a particular topic, usually one that you introduced when you established the context for the circle. Use the timer to set 3-4 minute for each woman's share so that everyone gets an equal chance. And make sure to stick to the timer! 3-4 minutes may seem like it would feel rushed, but the truth is, you'll notice that women typically finish a few seconds before the bell goes off. Knowing ahead of time how long you have to share helps you be intentional and get to the point.

Element 5: Guided Break

Instead of just allowing everyone to disperse, I find it helpful to "contain" the break by asking everyone to get up and do some movement together. There are several great ways to facilitate movement. A simple one is to just put on a song and have everyone dance.

Another fun exercise you might try is called "follow the leader," where the circle leader starts the dance movements. I make them very simple, just to get women moving playfully. Everyone joins in, doing exactly what the circle leader does, and after you've done a couple moves, you point to the next woman, who creates the next dance moves for everyone to join, and so on until the song stops. I think this is the best way to do a movement break. If you're already a movement facilitator, this is your time to shine!

Element 6: Additional Content

This is an optional element where you might have more content, such as paired shares, a second round of group share, journaling, or a ritual that embodies the intention of the circle.

FORM THE MASCULINE CONTAINER

Element 7: Closing Ceremony

The closing can be as simple as blowing out a candle to signify that circle is complete and that sacred space is now closed, or you can do any other type of ritual of your choosing.

As you can see, the structure is basic. As I mentioned earlier, our goal with the structure is KISS: keep it simple, sweetheart. The key is in creating safety and sacredness. Circle is a place to open up and get real, it's not a place to come and gossip or talk about shopping and the weather. These structural elements help maintain the integrity of the circle and create the experience of a safe sacred space.

Of course, there are many nuances to structure beyond this overall shape, so let's go over the top five frequently asked questions about structuring a circle.

FAQs

1: How do I structure my circle for a small group of women?

If you have a smaller circle, less than twelve women, I highly recommend that you create a large group sharing experience where every single woman in the circle gets to share with the group as a whole. To do this, divide up the time depending on how many women are there and how much time you've allotted in your circle outline for sharing. Have each woman do a share from two to four minutes, which is plenty of time for each woman to share fully.

When they have only a few minutes to speak, most women get to the point and what they say is so much more powerful. That woman's share may then inspire the other women, who start to have their own

THE ART OF LEADING CIRCLE

insights on the same topic. One woman might not have any idea what she's going to share before the woman next to her shares, and then after listening to her neighbor's share, she has this huge epiphany that sparks her own share.

Also, as a circle leader, I personally do not let anyone skip out. There's something really powerful that happens for a woman when she initially doesn't want to share, but does anyway. Perhaps she feels vulnerable or is afraid of what others will think. When she shares no matter what, she has this new experience of being able to speak her truth, which builds self-esteem and self-acceptance.

Also, when women share despite their resistance and tap into emotion because they share something vulnerable, it opens up the whole space, giving other women permission to go deep as well. The bonding that occurs when there is deep authentic sharing is unparalleled. When you hear someone's pain or triumph and can relate, you feel connected. This is what creates real sisterhood. Women *get* that they aren't alone, and that it's not only safe to be vulnerable, but that vulnerability alleviates stress and lifts your mood.

To complement the group share, paired shares are a very valuable tool in circle because they develop 1:1 intimacy. It's amazing how women get paired with the perfect partner and they discover common threads with one another.

2: How do I structure my circle for large groups of women, say 20+?

Since a whole group share for a large group of women would likely take up your entire circle time, I highly recommend a ritual called "Puja Style Circle Sharing" if you have a large group, usually any more than twelve women. For Puja Style Circle Sharing, create a larger outer

FORM THE MASCULINE CONTAINER

circle of women and an inner circle of women, facing each other so that each woman in the inner circle is matched up with a woman on the outer circle.

You create a question prompt for each round of sharing. When both women in each pair finish the first round, the inner circle rotates clockwise so everyone has a new partner. After they switch, have them introduce themselves again and give everyone a new question. You can also mix up what you ask each pair to do: you could ask a question for one pair, and then an activity for the next, like a massage or eye gazing. Get creative with the content!

Puja Style Circle Sharing is ideal for large groups. In fact, I've had as many as forty women share in circle this way, which is a great way to create a lot of energy in the space and have them be able to connect with as many people as possible. The women will continue rotating for a set amount of time; with a really large group, Puja Style sharing could be a full hour.

3: How do you lead a paired share effectively, especially when there are lots of women talking?

The three tools you need to handle this situation are a timer, a bell, and clear instructions.

The louder the bell, the better, because you don't want to yell. I remember one circle I led with over thirty women when I forgot my bell; it was a disaster trying to get everyone to switch. It was like herding cats.

Here's an sample script illustrating how to use these tools to facilitate a paired share:

THE ART OF LEADING CIRCLE

Okay, get into your pairs and say hello to your partner. Now everyone, please stop and look up here so you can hear the instructions. You're going to have two minutes each. The woman with the longest hair gets to go first.

Whoever is going first, please raise your hand. Here's the question to prompt your share: _____. You're going to wrap up when you hear the bell. The second person will then share while you listen. When you are listening, please give your undivided attention to your partner and do not interrupt or give any feedback. Simply hold space for them.

Put on the timer once you've finished giving instructions. When the timer goes off, ring the bell and ask everyone to stop. Because they are talking, you may need to be loud, but the bell will help you get their initial attention since you've already let them know to listen for it.

Then, give the second partner a cue to start as you start the timer. When the timer goes off for the second time, ring the bell and say: *We're complete, everyone. Thank your partner and give them a hug.*

Don't be surprised if youI have to repeat this final instruction a couple of times. In paired sharing, it's especially important to stay on top of the timer and give clear vocal instructions.

4: Do I have to have movement in my circle? What if I'm a terrible dancer or the women don't want to dance?

Movement is important to shift the energy of circle. It can be used to release intense emotions or to bring the energy up, and can also be used to get women out of their heads.

If you are a terrible dancer or feel awkward leading, "follow the leader" (described earlier) works like a charm every time. Your dance moves

FORM THE MASCULINE CONTAINER

can be as simple and playful as you want, like "Staying Alive." And although you want to make sure everyone participates in the shares, if someone doesn't want to dance, then just let her disappear into the bathroom. She's still moving and shifting her energy.

5: What's the difference between visualization and meditation? How do I lead one?

A visualization is you talking the women through what you want them to see or what you want them to evoke. For example, you encourage them to visualize entering a garden and meeting their inner child. They may play with their inner child and ask what their inner child wants to say to them. After a visualization, you can have them journal, draw, or get into a paired share or a group share and talk about what they saw and experienced.

A meditation is where you guide the women to connect to themselves, but not using visual cues to take them on a journey. They are not using their imagination or seeing what image comes to their mind. In my circles, I use meditations at the beginning to help ground the women and have them become present. There might be a forgiveness meditation, where I guide them through talking about forgiveness and how to feel that in their body.

There is a link in the Resources Section at the back of the book to two bundles of Sistership Circle meditations and their scripts. I suggest that you listen to some first to get the idea and then use your creativity to make one yourself.

What's wonderful about the overall circle structure is that you can use all these different elements and put them together to create a unique experience for your circle. However, be careful not to put too much

THE ART OF LEADING CIRCLE

into your circle. Remember that less is more, even when it comes to circling. Sometimes we create this really lengthy agenda and it's just too much. The circle can become overloaded. Keep it simple. Simple can create massive change because it creates space for what wants to come through, which is the principle of the feminine flow. The concept of the feminine will guide the energetics of your circle: who you're being and the space you're holding as the facilitator, to create authentic connection.

3

Trust the Feminine Flow

*"A Woman in harmony with her spirit is like
a river flowing. She goes where she will without
pretense and arrives at her destination prepared
to be herself and only herself."*
~ *Maya Angelou*

The previous section dealt with the structure of a circle, which is the masculine aspect of circle. Now let's talk about the energetics of a circle, which is the feminine aspect.

Energy held in a solid structure that has integrity, with no leaks, can start to spiral upward, raising the vibration of the women and literally filling them up. I don't know how many times I've left circle feeling quite high, and had a hard time going to sleep when I got home. That experience is energy: the feminine magic, the connection, the co-

THE ART OF LEADING CIRCLE

creation, the intuition, the creativity, the Shakti, the life force of the circle.

> One of our facilitators asked me once: "What do you think is your secret sauce to being an effective facilitator?" My answer is simple: just falling in love with the women. Can you allow yourself to fall in love with the women in your circle right away, in just a couple hours?

In order to be able to do that, first you have to come from a place of self love, really loving yourself as a facilitator, as a woman, as who you are in your essence and who you are in your unique strengths and weaknesses. When you love all parts of yourself, you can then extend that love and bring it out to the other women in the circle.

Second, you set the intention for a judgment free, open space for women to just be themselves. This is what is called holding space: making sure that you are this clear vessel holding the energy of the circle. Creating your structure for circle helps to create a container, but the energetics of that container are in the way you hold space for these women to be whoever they need to be and to say whatever they need to say.

TRUST THE FEMININE FLOW

As the circle facilitator, you're really just loving them as they are: without judgment, in full acceptance and clarity. You're not bringing in your baggage to the experience. You're literally emptied out, so that you can just hold the space and be fully present to whatever needs to happen in the circle.

The next important energetic piece to holding the container is being vulnerable and allowing yourself to *be* wherever you're at. You don't have to pretend to be anything other than yourself, right here, right now. You don't need to act a certain way. What's made me so successful as a facilitator is that I've let that go. I do not need to put on a happy face. If I've been having a bad day, I can vulnerably share that something happened to me. It's important to clarify that this is not me dumping that into the space and creating a heavy energy for everyone, but instead this is me leading from my vulnerability and creating the space for other women to also do the same. This is really just leading by example. If I want sacredness, then I'm going to treat myself as sacred-- *all* parts of myself. If I want vulnerability, then I'm going to lead with vulnerability. If I want authenticity, then I'm going to be authentic and I'm not going to pretend to be someone I'm not. I'm going to show up as me.

Of course, as the facilitator, you're balancing this with holding space for everyone. You don't want to come in with a bunch of baggage, but if you had a bad morning or your dog died, you don't want to pretend that didn't happen, either, because that wouldn't be showing up as your sacred, vulnerable, authentic self. You want to use whatever is going on as an opportunity to open up the space and have everyone else be able to share anything that is weighing on their heart from earlier in that day.

THE ART OF LEADING CIRCLE

The two main energetic components of the circle are being yourself in a space of love, and holding space for whatever wants to happen.

If you are wondering, what if I can't handle what wants to happen? What if someone has heavy stuff come up and gets super emotional? How do I handle that? This is where advanced training comes in to help you to go deeper within yourself, because the deeper you go within yourself, the deeper that you can hold safe space.

If you are afraid of what might happen and how to handle something, here's the basic thing that you need to know: You don't need to do anything. You don't need to "fix" what's happening. It's not your job to coach, either. You are there to simply hold space and to allow women to have their experience as it is.

Now that is the hard part of leading circle, right? You may be thinking: how do I not take it personally? How do I hold that space without bringing all my stuff in?

This is the power of the feminine. We must trust ourselves and trust the medicine of the circle. It's mysterious and unknown at times. This is where the Advanced Level 2 and 3 training at Sistership Circle comes in.

Let's pause for a moment and take a deep breath. This is a tool I frequently use and that I'd like to teach you right now. When you get tight and tense, frozen because you don't know what to do, take a breath. If you feel the room get tight and tense, ask everyone to take a deep breath with you.

This fear of the unknown is probably the number one thing that holds you back from getting started, but you've got to start somewhere. And trust me: God, Goddess, Universe is not going to give you anything that you cannot handle. You are going to get exactly what you can handle, exactly what you need for your own growth and development as a facilitator. So really, there's no failure, because there's nothing you can lose. There's no way that you can possibly do it wrong. You're going to do it perfectly, exactly where you're at on your journey.

Circle can go deep, and that's a good thing. In order to take care of yourself as you grow your capacity to hold deep space, one tool you may find helpful is working with feminine leader archetypes like The Mother.

Featured Facilitator: Lisa Stromsmoe

Accessing a mix of masculine and feminine qualities when planning for a circle will save you so much energy. We all have masculine and feminine qualities within us. One set of qualities is usually more dominant than the other depending on the person. However, without one, the other cannot reach its full potential. They support one another. And that is the beauty of circle. We're always discovering ways we can do things differently to magnetize amazing women into our circles.

For a while, I invited women to circle without any structure. It felt like I was always doing things last minute. After every circle, I would get sick for days. This happened every month for the first four months I facilitated circles. I considered stopping because I already had so much on my plate. I thought that the unwanted pressure on my body was not worth it. Thankfully my why for wanting circle in my life was much stronger than my resistance.

I realized that a lot of the tasks I did each month were duplicatable. So, I set up a system where I could literally copy and paste the structure of the circle each month and change the details depending on the theme. This system was also scalable,

THE ART OF LEADING CIRCLE

meaning that most of the tasks were able to be completed by someone other than me. This allowed me to be the invitation and in the feminine flow.

Visualize the masculine and feminine supporting one another like a river system. The masculine qualities are the river banks - the structure, direction, and processes. The feminine qualities are the water features - the depth, flow, and swirls. The feminine feels safe and protected by the landscape that is provided to her by the masculine. It becomes easier to reach her potential destination, even with all of the whirling that happens along the way (imagine eddies and rapids), because she no longer has to worry about how things are going to happen.

The masculine is the "doing" and creates structure. The feminine is the "being" and creates connections. The combination of both creates more harmony in your life when planning for circles. It also creates a more balanced brand and image that attracts women with different dominant aspects within themselves. Touching on both masculine and feminine qualities during your process sends the signal of wholeness - all aspects are welcome.

Activate the Bonding Hormone as the Mother

"Women most certainly carry a more sympathetic heart in the traditional, classic sense of the mother archetype. They have been given the role to carry the heart energy of the human community, whereas men carry the survival energy."
~ Caroline Myss

There are four main feminine leader archetypes that we work with at Sistership Circle: the Mother, the Priestess, the Wise Woman, and the Queen.

According to Jungian psychology, archetypes are recurrent symbols or motifs in literature, art, or mythology, but they are also energies that reside within all of us, regardless of age, life experience, or personality. Each of us carries these energies within our unconscious; they become

THE ART OF LEADING CIRCLE

more fully activated and understood through our life experience and intentions, as well as when we focus on them directly.

It's like having a blueprint within us, like our genetics: many genes are present, but the environment determines how and when a certain gene gets expressed and at what level.

The Mother is the embodiment of a safe space for the deepest conversations and revealing deepest shame. She is the warm, soft marshmallow blanket of love. The nurturer, full of compassion, connection and generosity, she helps people feel seen, heard, and valued. The Mother listens with unconditional love and acceptance. Her presence is grounded, warm, inviting and safe. She invites connection and makes everyone feel like they belong, as if all women are her daughters who can just crawl up on her lap and be held.

I've mentioned several times that connection creates safety. Connection is the reason that women come to circle in the first place. The more that you as a circle leader are attuned to this need to connect, the better you can respond. A common pitfall as a facilitator is to act the role of the teacher, attached to a circle outline to teach the women something. But this is not why we come to circle. That's why we go to a workshop, or read a book like this one.

All the healing and transformation instead occurs when women feel connected. In early childhood, we have one major need above all else and that is to feel loved. But most of us did not receive unconditional love. I've heard hundreds, if not thousands, of women say how disconnected they were from their mothers, how they did not feel seen, heard, or loved growing up. Circle then becomes that safe haven where women can finally experience the love that was missing for so many years.

ACTIVATE THE BONDING HORMONE AS THE MOTHER

As the circle leader, you have an opportunity to embody the mother archetype in her healthy qualities of unconditional love, support, and acceptance; to heal those old mother wounds simply in who you are being as you hold space. The mother archetype helps you do that with a very powerful tool: activating the bonding hormone, oxytocin.

In *Psychology Today*[1], Paul Zak writes: "The 'love molecule,' oxytocin, is the chemical foundation for trusting others. Activated by positive social interactions, it makes us care about others in tangible ways, and it motivates us to work together for a common purpose."

Based on Zak's advice, here are seven things you can do to increase the oxytocin in the room and create greater connection in the circle:

1. Make eye contact when you are listening.

2. Give a gift.

3. Share a meal. This is one reason to start circle with a potluck!

4. Create meditations that allow the women to focus on each other.

5. Create an activity that is moderately stressful. When we go through a challenging experience with someone and make it to the other side, we feel more bonded to them.

6. Tell your sisters you love them.

7. Hug. Touch not only raises oxytocin, but also reduces cardiovascular stress and can improve the immune system, too.

---

[1] https://www.psychologytoday.com/us/blog/the-moral-molecule/201311/the-top-10-ways-boost-good-feelings

THE ART OF LEADING CIRCLE

With all these tools, you'll lead circles that flow from the divine feminine while being held by the sacred masculine. Equally important to what happens in the circle, however, is what happens afterward.

Featured Facilitator: Maria Huerta

My mom died when I was 7 years old and I grew up surrounded by my dad and five siblings. My dad was like a hen with his wings always open to protect and love his children. The mother role was shared between my older sisters and my dad. The love, compassion, inspiration for autonomy, and freedom that a mother gives us came to me in a divided way through my father and my sisters, but I always felt the absence of my mother and longed for the unique and articulated source of love and connection the mother can provide.

Life made me become a mother at 16, and so, I wanted to be the mother I never had for my daughter. We grew up together, and then I had more children for whom my greatest desire was to be the conscious and full mom I didn't have. In my own personal growth, I later learned to become that mom for myself.

The Mother archetype has been established in me forever, to the point that the choice of my profession as a psychologist was influenced by it. As Osho says, "A good therapist must be immensely compassionate, because it is not his techniques of therapy that help people, it is his love." And for me, that is the truth.

When I started facilitating circles, I realized that circle is a new space of love where I can give expression to this archetype. I do face-to-face circles in my house, and each circle begins by welcoming women to the sacred space of my home where we share a cup of tea, coffee, or water in the kitchen, and where I share with them the magic of having (literally) hundreds of plants inside my house. There is always someone who wants to have a space like this and then I offer them a little piece of a plant and the secrets of how to make them grow and flourish in the same way they do in my house.

ACTIVATE THE BONDING HORMONE AS THE MOTHER

Physical contact is one of my greatest ways of expressing love. Thus, my circles, whether in Spanish or English, are full of hugs and touch. The women in my circles feel that they belong and are accepted as themselves.

On Mother's Day, a woman from circle wrote to me: "Happy Mother's Day, beautiful Maria! For being a mother! And also for bringing that feeling of motherhood and sorority to all the women you guide and accompany in circle, so we can discover ourselves as creators on this Earth! Enjoy your day!"

For me, the Mother archetype helps me enter into a deep connection with women. It gives me the opportunity to give unconditional love and to feel compassion. I take pleasure in the essence of motherhood, now extended to the women who walk beside me. From this mother's love, I offer the opportunity to give and receive that love, and in this way, we nurture each other in circle.

5

Integrate After Circle

"My mother always says people should be able to take care of themselves, even if they're rich and important."
~ Frances Hodgson Burnett, The Secret Garden

Once you complete your circle, it's really important that you carve out the time and space for integration. The "after care" is just as important as the prep and the facilitation. Sometimes, you may feel like you have a circle hangover: you are exhausted, wiped out and drained. Other times you may feel on top of the world.

Either experience is valid. Whatever you feel, I want to share with you the best way to process your circle afterward, so that you get the lessons from circle and can apply them to the next one, making them better and better each time.

THE ART OF LEADING CIRCLE

> "Water is a wonderful element to cleanse and release any energy you may have picked up from the circle."

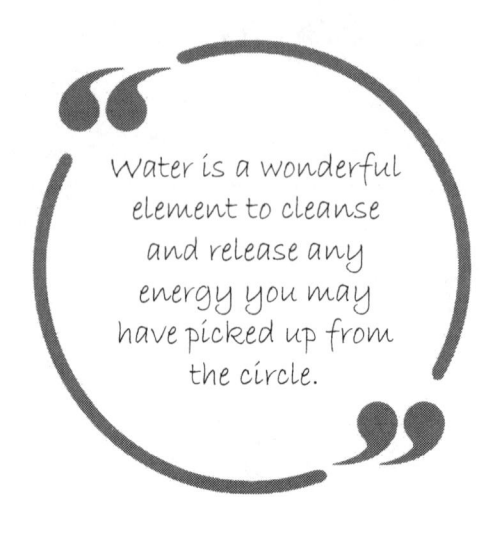

The best way I have found to integrate what happened in circle is through the element of water, like in a bubble bath or shower. Water is a wonderful element to cleanse and release any energy you may have picked up from the circle. It's a very healing way to let your mind sort through things, but also to let your body just relax and celebrate. You've done it! You led your circle.

Every circle that you hold is a huge accomplishment. Every circle is a huge contribution to the women who showed up, and that ripples out to their families and friends. Make time to do something nurturing and relaxing to celebrate and recalibrate. Take care of yourself. You deserve it.

The next thing to think about is what if the circle went really deep? What if some women revealed some really dark stuff? When you first start facilitating, you might have the tendency of taking on the energy of the circle. The long-term practice is in *not* taking on the energy of circle and learning how to keep yourself clean and clear. But if you do take on some of the energy, it's important to have support structures in place to process anything that triggered you.

One helpful practice is to move your body after circle. You can ground your energy by getting into your thighs, with a movement like horse stance or a wall sit, and then discharge the energy with a movement like shaking.

INTEGRATE AFTER CIRCLE

Once your energy is clear, the next step is to take inventory and evaluate how the circle went. First, look at what worked and went well. Practice having love and compassion for yourself. Learn to celebrate yourself and not beat yourself up.

Take inventory and rate yourself in a way that's empowering versus disempowering. Give yourself credit and be compassionate with yourself. We have a worksheet available to do this in the Art of Leading Circle Startup Kit.

Once you feel grounded and have done your evaluation, take the key lessons and follow up with your participants with whatever communication you prefer to use: text, email, Facebook messenger, etc. Get in touch with the women within 24 hours to keep the connection alive.

In your message, first and foremost, thank them for coming. If you have a reading or quote from circle, share that. If you took a photo, share that. If you have your next gathering date, share that as well.

Ask them how the experience was for them, and if they have any feedback for you. Participant feedback helps you improve. We provide a feedback form in the Startup Kit.

If you have not created one yet, I encourage you to create a Facebook group and invite the women to continue the conversation, so that they have a space to process or share what maybe didn't get shared at circle or what comes up for them post-circle. Stuff is always going to come up afterwards for women. And it's so good for you to welcome that process, through that first message, so that they know step-by-step where they can go to continue the healing, sharing, and connecting.

THE ART OF LEADING CIRCLE

When you provide that continued connection, it's almost like they never leave circle. And the best way for you to get the discussion started outside of circle is by initiating it yourself. This follow up is HUGE for building relationships and establishing your circle community.

The follow up is also a critical component to have women come back to circle again. The continued connection creates a relationship, and they will be able to see clearly how much you genuinely care. Don't get lazy with this part. The rewards are worth it when the women who have participated feel connected to you and to the circle.

Now that we've been through how to create a safe container for circle, let's take a closer look at how to hold the space you've just created.

Featured Facilitator: Kalika Sharma

As a circle facilitator, I look forward to integration after a circle as much as I look forward to facilitating circles themselves. Firstly, after a circle, making time with myself for integration is key, which means closing the doors to distractions and others' voices for a little bit so I can identify what's going on with me. It's best to sit down and journal during this time and let the feelings and thoughts flow on paper, which helps me integrate specific things like what's working and what isn't so I can do better in the future.

Secondly, integration after a circle also means a time of rest, because I do work myself up quite a bit, especially the night before the circle. After the circle is complete, I can truly relax and take in what has happened, what went according to plan and what didn't.

Third, knowing my strengths and weaknesses and being brave enough to face my shadow each time is part of my own personal integration in my life as well as integration in circle. For the most part, I don't see the two as very different things.

INTEGRATE AFTER CIRCLE

A couple of themes have shown up repeatedly with me, and I have been integrating them over a period of two years of facilitating circles. Those themes are working with opening up a receiving block and also integrating a more structured masculine side of myself.

As for my receiving block, I started off facilitating circles in Mumbai, India when my capacity to receive anything at all was cut off. I felt "altruistic" about facilitating, but I was unable to have women who attended circles support me in any way. Even if there was love and support for me, I felt very uncomfortable receiving it. I couldn't even see what I was receiving. I thought I was being radical and not really bothering about creating a community, but the truth is that because I keep facing my shadow, I know that I didn't feel I deserve a community I built. I still keep going back to these struggles to integrate one circle at a time.

As for integrating a more structure masculine side of myself, "feminine flow" comes more naturally to me and I don't particularly like too much structure in my circles. So after a circle, during my integration time, I try to look for the places where I could improve on the more masculine side that I struggle with. With each circle, I reflect on my own capacity for holding a container without letting it drop at any point, in case I fall into fear at any point. Post-facilitation, I'm integrating a more organized, planned, and goal-oriented masculine side of myself.

Integration after a circle is a journey for any facilitator and circles are a great mirror of your own soul integration; I feel blessed to keep uncovering new sides of me through this work.

Hold Sacred Space as the Priestess

*"Holding Space means that we are willing to walk alongside
another person in whatever journey they're on without judging them,
making them feel inadequate, trying to fix them, or trying to impact
the outcome. When we hold space for other people, we open our hearts, offer
unconditional support, and let go of judgement and control."*
~ Heather Plett

Creating a safe space in circle is clearly important, but it's equally important to create a sacred space. One of the things that distinguishes the women's circles we are creating is that we make the experience of circle sacred, meaning spiritual in nature.

Sacred circle does not have chattiness or cattiness. Women are dropped in and present in their bodies. They see circle as a revered space for healing and transformation. They honor the space because they see it as something very, very special.

THE ART OF LEADING CIRCLE

One of my favorite energetic tools to create this sense of sacredness is connecting with the energy of various feminine leader archetypes. If you'd like, there's a quiz in the Resource Section that will identify which of the four main archetypes is strongest within you.

The archetype we're going to focus on now is the Priestess, the keeper of the temple. As the one who performs ritual, she is the sacred space holder for circle. The Priestess channels spirit and then serves from her heart. She holds space for transformation. Embodying the Priestess is about finding that intersection between spirit from Father Sky from above and space with Mother Earth: she is the integration of masculine and feminine.

One of the most important aspects of the Priestess when it comes to leading circle is creating and holding ritual and sacred space. The key question then becomes, how do you create sacredness?

> There are three steps: silence, presence, and ritual.

The first step is creating an atmosphere of silence. When the women enter the space where circle will be held, ask them to walk in silence, perhaps lighting a candle when they enter the space. They are crossing over the threshold into the circle room the way they would enter a temple: with reverence and honor for themselves and those around them. You may need to explain the significance of the silent entrance so they understand and honor the space.

The second step to creating sacredness for circle is holding that sacredness within yourself, the circle leader, as the Priestess. This doesn't mean that you have to be stern, but that you embody and exude seriousness and full presence.

The third step is moving through ritual, which is any type of action that's put in a prescribed order or sequence of events. Each woman who enters the space moves through the ritual.

There are so many rituals to work with! Sistership Circle has created multiple Ritual Handbooks for various seasons, themes, and events. Their links are available in the Resource Section.

At Sistership Circle, we have an opening ceremony and a licensed opening invocation that our certified Sistership Circle facilitators use to open their circles. We perform the same "Stitching" ritual at the beginning of every circle to add a layer of consistency.

Of course, when you have the same ritual to start your circle every single time, it's easy to unconsciously run through the motions, which is how a ritual loses its sacredness. That's why it's important when you do any ritual, for the first time or the hundredth time, to infuse it with as much intention and reverence and honoring as possible. Treat the ritual like it is sacred, because it is. Treat it with consciousness: be aware of yourself and how moving through the ritual feels in your body.

I've read our opening invocation hundreds of times. And still, when I really tap into the words, it makes me cry, because I feel it with my

THE ART OF LEADING CIRCLE

whole heart. That's what you want to do: *feel* the ritual every single time that you do it and don't allow yourself to go through it unconsciously.

Your own opening ceremony should include at least these three things: a welcome, grounding meditation, and connection. The welcome is an intentional ritual, such as lighting a candle or saging each woman. The grounding meditation is meant to leave everything else in life outside of the circle, to clear away everything else. The connection is heart to heart, such as looking eye to eye and giving hugs.

Let's say you've led circle a few times, and now the women know each other, so when they arrive, they want to socialize and it becomes harder for them to drop into sacred space. How do you maintain the sacredness and continue to hold the space as the Priestess?

The answer starts with healing the part of you that is afraid of taking a stand. Often, healing this part means taking a look at your relationship with women in the past and what we call the Sister Wound.

For example, in high school, I was always afraid that if I spoke my truth, if I really held agreements, if I stood in my integrity, I would be known as a bitch and that people wouldn't like me. And that same story would come up for me whenever I felt like I needed to hold the integrity of the circle, say, by moving women past the initial chattiness. I would tend to get lax because I didn't want anyone to not like me. When I identified this story from the past and saw that it was blocking my facilitation, that awareness allowed me to find the strength to change the story.

I used the same mantra I mentioned in talking about the How to Lead Circle Blueprint to identify my fear and the limiting belief underneath:

INTEGRATE AFTER CIRCLE

"This is not who I am, this is what I learned. And if I learned it, I can unlearn it."

When you have awareness of where the story is coming from, you can then reframe and change the story. The truth is, you can maintain integrity in a way that women honor and respect you.

Embodying the archetype of the Priestess can give you the strength to do this as a facilitator. The Priestess heals whatever is in the way of being a channel for the truth to come through her. The Priestess is courageous in holding the container, holding up the integrity, and speaking truth in the space.

Of course, sometimes this means that, as circle leader, you may have to call someone out. Obviously, you want to do this lovingly, but in a way that firmly upholds the integrity of the safe and sacred space.

For example, if women are chatting away and it's time to start, you might say:

Ladies, we're about to start, and I understand that you want to connect with each other and talk. But right now this is sacred circle space and we're going to remain in our sacredness and we're going to hold our chatter and our jokes until after the circle. So if you ladies would hold that with me, I would really appreciate it. How does that feel for you? Are you all ready?

See how this gentle reminder comes from a place of honoring the women in the circle *and* honoring the integrity of the circle? As a facilitator, you're coming from a place of compassion and love, but also standing in the truth and in integrity.

THE ART OF LEADING CIRCLE

Earlier in the book, we talked about feminine leadership and how there are three main distinctions: being the example, leading from your feminine super powers, and co-creating in collaboration with others. The Priestess leads by modeling and being the example.

Featured Facilitator: Youmna Zein

As I entered into the vast world of spirituality, one of the biggest mysteries to me was the notion of Sacred Space. Coming from a highly technical engineering background, holding Sacred Space to me made as much sense as thinking about the sun rising from the west.

How do you hold Sacred Space?

What does "sacred" even mean?

That was where I started. I decided to embark on an inner journey to truly understand what Sacred meant to me. I deliberately say "to me" because I very quickly realized it was a very individual and unique journey that is quite different for each of us.

What was revealed to me as I began my exploration was that the concept of Sacredness is truly inseparable from all aspects of life. Indeed, Sacred is all that stems from the Divine, the Universe, Oneness - whatever is the word you choose to describe the Source of this infinite creation. That meant that life itself is Sacred. The very breath that you inhale and exhale is Sacred. The land, the water, the fire, the air are all Sacred. In fact, every atom, every cell, every existence in this dimension and beyond is Sacred. Both good and bad, joy and pain, life and death are all Sacred. For in truth, the notion of Sacredness rises above that duality. In the realms of the Sacred, everything just is.

One of the most powerful experiences that allowed me to tap deeper into Sacredness was when I began participating in and facilitating Sistership Circles. I remember

INTEGRATE AFTER CIRCLE

clearly my first circle experience, where I had assumed I was merely joining a group of women to share experiences and relate to each other. My mind was blown, to say the least, by the level of honoring and reverence to the process of circling and to the circle space that I experienced.

It was in circle that I truly saw the physical manifestation of Sacredness and holding Sacred Space.

In circle, every woman is a Goddess.

In circle, every emotion is an expression of Divine energy.

In circle, every ritual, every anointing oil, every meditation, is a channel to Source.

That is when it became clear to me what it meant to hold Sacred Space.

When a space is deemed Sacred, whether inside or outside of circle, it is an invitation to tap into the depths of the Universe and to experience a multi-dimensional reality. The difference between the presence or absence of Sacredness lies only in how much you choose to see beyond the veil of the physical world.

To hold Sacred Space is to see beyond the notion of separation and into Oneness, and to allow all who choose to step into the same space to experience their own Divinity with no judgment, no fear, no jealousy nor hatred, with only unconditional love. When holding Sacred Space, there is nothing you need to do, no one you need to be, nothing you need to say. In holding Sacred Space, you are Divine and so is every being in that space with you and that is all you need to remember.

Be the Example and Embody Feminine Leadership

"Vulnerability sounds like truth and feels like courage. Truth and courage aren't always comfortable, but they're never weakness."
~ Brené Brown

Remember that the three main pieces of the new model of feminine leadership: being the example, leading from your feminine superpowers, and co-creating in collaboration. We're going to do a deep dive into the first element, being the example, and the three things we specifically want to embody: vulnerability and truth-telling, co-creative leadership, and the law of receiving.

THE ART OF LEADING CIRCLE

Vulnerability

Creating a deep, authentic container for women to really have transformation starts with you and your vulnerability. You can only lead women as deep as you are personally willing to go. But vulnerability is considered a weakness in today's culture, and it is really hard for women to get vulnerable. We apologize for our tears and cover up our emotions. We keep ourselves "safe" by not allowing ourselves to be vulnerable, with ourselves or with others.

The truth is, circle is all about revealing yourself, which means you as the facilitator need to model what it looks like to get real so the other women not only have permission, but can see what it actually looks like (since chances are they haven't been taught in school or by their parents).

I want to share a few examples of times when I showed up to lead circle from a vulnerable place. The first was years back: my boyfriend and I were living together, and one day, he came home from work, sat down on the bed, and broke up with me. And I had circle that night. So I sat in my car for an hour beforehand and then walked into the space sobbing. The women held me while I cried and cried for about fifteen minutes. Finally, I stopped crying and said, "Ok, I'm ready to lead the circle now."

This is an example of me showing up in my mess, in no capacity to lead. But by allowing my emotions to flow, the energy moved and I was eventually able to come back to my center. That circle was so powerful because everyone was able to drop into a much deeper place. Can you imagine what might have happened if I had tried to ignore or bottle up what I was going through, and led circle from that place instead? Being vulnerable as a leader means being willing to be honest, with

BE THE EXAMPLE AND EMBODY FEMININE LEADERSHIP

yourself and with your circle, about where you're coming from, not keeping it to yourself.

Another example: once, when I was reading our opening invocation at circle, something triggered me halfway through. I burst into tears and had to stop reading. The women sat there and held space for me. I shared with them that I was feeling pretty tender from the day, and then brought it back to circle by saying, "This is what happens. This is feminine leadership and I'm not going to deny it. I'm just going to continue to hold the space in this soft tender place tonight."

The key in both of these examples is that I was able to go into the emotion, fully feel it, and create a lesson from it. I didn't dump on the women in attendance, and I wasn't putting negative energy into the space. One of those women continues to tell me to this day how much that moment impacted her, where she got to see me in my true authenticity. She said it helped her become more vulnerable in circle. Again, it was a beautiful circle that night.

I also had another incident with a virtual circle that I led on forgiveness; as I did a reading from my book, I started crying. When I finished, one of the women said, "You know, I wasn't quite sure about you. You've led circle so many times. And I thought maybe you were running through the motions. But I just got to see your humanity and I got to see how much this means to you. I got to see how you bring your full heart and soul into this work."

There's nothing wrong with crying in circle. There's nothing wrong with feeling sad in circle. There is no specific emotion that you need to be or should be demonstrating in circle. You just need to be authentic with whatever is coming up for you. And when you are vulnerable and get emotional, you express it in a way that doesn't dump on everyone

THE ART OF LEADING CIRCLE

else. You are not complaining or asking for advice or solutions. You're simply feeling it, allowing the emotion to move through you. From that point you can look for the lesson to share, making it as universal as possible to create permission and an opening for everyone else to go deeper into what's authentically there for them in the present moment.

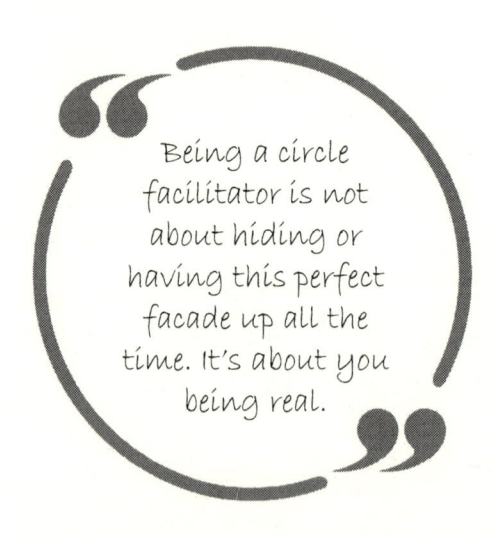

> Being a circle facilitator is not about hiding or having this perfect facade up all the time. It's about you being real.

What you'll find is that a lot of the time, whatever's happening in your space is what's happening in the group space. If you're feeling kind of off, chances are there's at least one other woman who's also feeling a little bit off. When you drop into your own feelings, you also tune into the group energy. Being a circle facilitator is not about hiding or having this perfect facade up all the time. It's about you being real. That's what circle itself is all about.

When you master this, leading with your vulnerability in a way that's providing permission and creating more space, you will have circles that are contagious. Women will want more because there is simply nothing else out there like it. Women are craving meaningful relationships, and being vulnerable with each other is how we get to those relationships.

The more that you feel, the deeper the container you can hold. Being vulnerable with yourself gives you access to holding space. You can fall apart in a minute and then bring yourself back together again. And yes, doing this can be intense and can feel edgy and very confronting, because this is something that women are afraid to step into in their

BE THE EXAMPLE AND EMBODY FEMININE LEADERSHIP

feminine leadership. And again, this takes practice and courage. But when you do it, you build confidence. And, most importantly, when you step into this place of vulnerability, you're being an example for the women in circle to do the same.

Featured Facilitator: Mary Rives

According to Brene Brown, the world's leading expert on the subject, vulnerability involves risk, uncertainty, and emotional exposure.

When we call women together for circle or invite a woman to spend time with us, we are taking risks. We risk being seen as we truly are, whether we're being authentic or upholding the image of how we wish to be seen. We risk being rejected. We risk what it takes to experience a true connection with ourselves and others. We risk being loved and accepted—and receiving that love and acceptance.

As challenging as all of the above can be, not taking risks, not leaping into the void of uncertainty, and being unwilling to share our feelings often comes at quite a cost. In exchange for staying in our comfort zone, we're far less likely to actualize our dreams, passions, and visions which translates into leading an unfulfilling life.

For me, even though my long-held dream was to become a transformational workshop facilitator, I let self-doubt, the fear of being seen and judged, and a family tragedy stop me for far too long.

At the age of 40 as a graduate school student, I remember feeling so excited to take an elective course in workshop facilitation. This was exactly what I'd been deeply desirous of for years. Just when I was about to present my first workshop, our best family friend (and my former lover), Woody, was brutally murdered.

My heart and family were devastated, but with encouragement and support, I miraculously managed to graduate. In the process, though, I dropped the workshop facilitation course. I used the tragic event of Woody's murder as a valid reason not to take the risk of becoming the powerful group leader I had previously envisioned myself to be. What a cop-out that was, a sad self-betrayal of stuffing down my heart's longing to lead groups.

On a more self-compassionate note, I was too shattered inside to even think of making myself vulnerable in front of a group of colleagues. That said, I did co-lead in the struggle for justice in Woody's honor, often bearing my heart and spilling my guts in emotional speeches I gave to the public, yet when it came to skillful group facilitation for the transformation of others, I simply wasn't ready, grounded, or focused enough—yet.

Fast forward 20 years. With the same dream lying dormant inside and trusting in divine timing, I found the way to finally activate it—or the way found me. My path brought me to Sistership Circle in 2018 and I'll soon complete my third circle facilitation training program (Mastery of Circle). It's through Sistership Circle's abundant leadership opportunities that I get to flex my muscles of courage to take risks, to practice being vulnerable and emotionally exposed, and model this for others in my training programs and circles.

Even after I become a certified Master Facilitator, I know I'll still have insecurities and other issues. I'll sometimes question if women will want what I have to offer, if they will ever come to "know, like, and trust" me. But not knowing if I'll be accepted, rejected, judged, or even get triggered no longer stops me from taking the risks because this is where my growing edges are, where the magic is.

By tuning in and going deep with our own shares, we give our sisters permission to be vulnerable and empower them to share courageously. The caveat here is that when we're in a leadership role, we don't use the group to heal us. Instead, we rely upon the therapeutic use of self-disclosure as the invitation.

BE THE EXAMPLE AND EMBODY FEMININE LEADERSHIP

Our vulnerability is an open invitation for women to see and trust that they are welcome to share deeply while being held, loved, respected, and accepted. This is the medicine and the magic. When we open our hearts and share what we really feel and think in such ways that enable the listener to receive our message, our deeper truths help us be seen and heard.

Being vulnerable doesn't come naturally to most of us. Over the course of our lifetime, we've had to defend and protect ourselves, sometimes for our very survival. For example, as a kid growing up with strict authoritarian parents, I discovered that if I lied my way out of sticky situations (of which there were plenty), I could actually spare myself from being gravely punished. For my safety, I could not afford to make myself vulnerable with the truth so I became a good liar, albeit not a pathological one. In adulthood, I'm grateful to have shifted to value and practice honesty, and in many moments, practicing radical honesty with compassion.

Those pesky defense mechanisms become incredibly clever and sophisticated. But if we practice making the conscious decision to choose courage over comfort and fear, being vulnerable and cultivating courage becomes easier and more natural. The rewards are worth the effort, worth feeling the fear, and being vulnerable anyway.

As you accept invitations to take risks, to be vulnerable, may you continue to find that the rewards far outshine the familiarity of your comfort zones so you can step into your true power and shine your light even brighter.

Co-Creative Leadership

The second aspect of being the example that's crucial for the new model of feminine leadership is co-creative leadership.

How often do you feel like you need to somehow prove yourself by doing it all by yourself? Proving our capabilities has been ingrained in

THE ART OF LEADING CIRCLE

us since childhood. If you've watched any toddler, they are constantly saying "I can do it myself!"

But in feminine leadership, we want to let go of this old individualistic model and instead embrace collaboration and co-creation. The truth is, you are not meant to do it alone. A circle cannot exist with just one person. As a facilitator, it is your job to enroll the women in the circle who then take full ownership of the circle. It becomes not just **your** circle but **our** circle.

Power is organized effort. For your circle to be powerful, for women to walk away transformed into feminine leaders and connected with one another in sisterhood beyond the scope of the circle itself, the group has to work together as a whole.

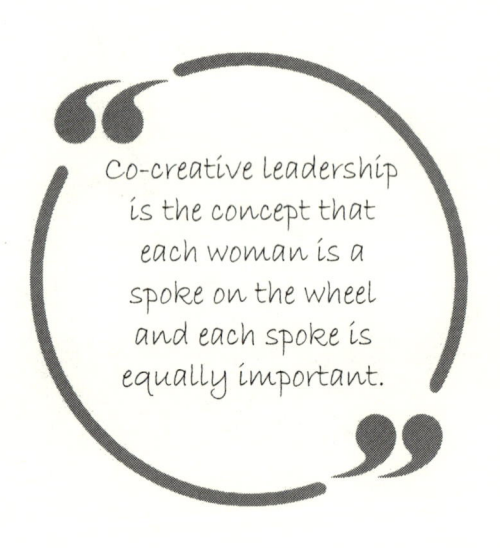

> Co-creative leadership is the concept that each woman is a spoke on the wheel and each spoke is equally important.

Co-creative leadership is the concept that each woman is a spoke on the wheel and each spoke is equally important. Each woman has her unique gifts and talents to bring to the group. Each woman is a contribution in and of herself. We don't have to do it all alone; we can focus on our strengths and allow others to bring their strengths so that together we are stronger and more powerful.

I burned out as a leader when I tried to do it all. I didn't trust that anyone could do it as well as I could, and I became resentful that I was giving my all and wasn't being appreciated or valued. The truth was, I wasn't allowing anyone to contribute *to* me, so I got stuck in the pattern

BE THE EXAMPLE AND EMBODY FEMININE LEADERSHIP

of doing everything before anyone else could even have a chance to contribute. But I found that the more I let go, the more women stepped into their power and received more value from the circle.

The idea that everyone is an equal contributor may seem to contradict the idea that you, the facilitator, should get paid to lead circle. However, that's simply not true. You are holding the space, no matter how co-creative in nature the circle is. Co-creative leadership is something you are modeling and women are learning how to do in circle.

It can feel really vulnerable to invite women into co-creative leadership. That's because we are not accustomed to it.

It's time to make a transition from ME to WE. In a culture dominated by independence and individuality, we are rarely taught how to have healthy, functional relationships within communities. We default to competition instead of collaboration.

This is why we lead circle: to model a new paradigm that will change the world!

Remember, each woman makes up the circle and it is important for everyone to own their value and worth in the circle. You matter. They matter. Your gifts matter. Their gifts matter. You've got to start by getting clear on what *you* have to contribute to the wheel of co-creative leadership and be the example for the women to follow your lead.

Answering the following questions will get you started on identifying and claiming your own contributions to co-created circles:

What are your innate gifts and abilities?

THE ART OF LEADING CIRCLE

What are your natural and developed talents?

What are you passionate about?

What are your strengths?

The following are also seven specific ways to have the women in your circle take ownership so you aren't doing it all yourself, creating more engagement and ease:

1. Set the Intention
Get clear from the beginning when you are starting your circle that the women will co-create the circle with you and everyone will embody their own leadership.

2. Get Agreement
Let the women know what it looks like to co-create the circle with you and to step into their leadership. Ask for their ideas and input.

3. Let them be responsible for their participation
Sometimes as leaders, we think we have to be responsible for everyone. Ask the women in your circle to take 100% responsibility for their participation.

4. Assign accountability
Ask someone to be the time keeper. Assign everyone to bring potluck dishes. Make someone the admin of your Facebook group. Whenever there is some request or action, ask who'd like to be in charge of it.

5. Give women the opportunity to lead or co-lead
In Sistership Circle, women get to co-lead some of our meetings. Ask the women in your circle to step up and lead the movement section or

BE THE EXAMPLE AND EMBODY FEMININE LEADERSHIP

the opening meditation. Ask women to find a partner and create an exercise for the group.

6. Ask for support
Being the leader doesn't mean you have to do all the set up or clean up. Ask the women to help you. If you are having a breakdown, be vulnerable and ask the circle to support you. Remember, you are facilitating by being the example.

7. Get feedback
What worked? What didn't work? Ask the circle to review your performance as a leader using a feedback form like the one in the Startup Kit.

Fully embracing these practices as the circle facilitator will set an example for the women in your circle as you all move towards the new model of co-creative leadership.

Featured Facilitator: Raffaella Bona

I applied Tanya's teachings around co-creative leadership when I organized a three-day retreat in the countryside around Berlin. It was supposed to be an offering I sold and led all by myself, but I put it out late, only a month before heading to the villa I booked. I was struggling to fill it up and feel ready to host it, as it was my very first one, so I did not manifest my clients.

I decided to instead turn my planned retreat into a co-creational weekend where each participant would cover their costs for transport, food, and accommodation, and would contribute with an activity of their preference, to share and practice their gifts and skills in a safe container, welcoming experiments.

THE ART OF LEADING CIRCLE

Well, in only two days I found five women eager to join me at the villa and everything went very smoothly from then on. It became not just my retreat but our retreat. We did not plan much in advance, only a few practical details and logistics, plus the potluck for the first evening, and as for the other meals, one of the women volunteered to cook for the group, as she is a professional chef. Perfect!

We each briefly mentioned the activity we would offer and we set up a meeting point and time at the train station and that was it. We left the rest to the Universe to take care of. We then spent a wonderful weekend together, surrounded by nature, taking care of ourselves, our bodies, hearts, and spirits, getting to know each other deeply in circle (the activity I offered), and sharing our unique gifts and talents.

Each woman facilitated a truly beautiful experience as an activity or play-shop that I would have never thought to do myself, from light language and essence discovery to intuitive dance and Dakini wisdom (sacred female spirits in Hinduism). We all learned and enjoyed them very much!

So, even though I did not earn any money from it, I gained so much, especially around the true meaning of co-creation and the beauty and ease of co-leading the overall experience, sharing the responsibilities, and leading tasks.

Everyone embodied her feminine leader and goddess within and we worked together as a connected group during the whole time together. Everything was flowing gracefully and there was no rush or worry about timing, planning, or scheduling, as we were in trust of the magic that our circle was bringing to us. We surrendered to retreating in sistership and the Universe provided some truly magical moments we will never forget.

And the best outcome is that we all left feeling empowered and worthy, confident and powerful, valued and appreciated, heard and seen, celebrated and loved.

BE THE EXAMPLE AND EMBODY FEMININE LEADERSHIP

The Law of Receiving

The final aspect of being the example that's so important for feminine leadership is understanding the law of receiving. The last thing you want to do as a facilitator is leave circle feeling burned out. Do you know the number one cause of circle burnout?

Overgiving.

Let's discuss the antidote to overgiving and how you can leave circle feeling filled up and more energized than when you came in.

At Sistership Circle, we teach a concept that may feel contrary to what you may already think of facilitation: you to come into the circle as a participant as well as a space holder. Balancing the two roles is something that you have to practice to become good at. But here's the easiest way to get started with this practice: Set an intention for your own growth and expansion in the circle. You created this circle not just for others, but also for your desire to have deeper connection and sisterhood in your life. You are in the circle to *receive* love, support, and contribution from your sisters, as well as to give.

You may initially have the mindset that holding space means that you separate yourself from the circle, but I believe that the opposite is actually what will create more sustainable energy for you.
I want to make a really important distinction before we move ahead: **there is a difference between receiving and taking**.

Taking is coming from scarcity, lack, fear, and a feeling of "I'm not enough." The energy of taking asks, "What am I going to get?" That mindset can have a heavy, draining energy on others. When you take, you deplete the energy of the group as well as your own energy.

THE ART OF LEADING CIRCLE

When you are taking, you are trying to make sure you get what you want from the circle.

When you are receiving, you are trusting, surrendering into the space that you will get what you need from the circle because the universe is always giving you exactly what you need and you are always taken care of. Receiving is a flow; it's the same thing as giving. When I ask for support and someone shows up for me, they are giving their time and energy. In return, they are receiving something for their contribution when they are willing and excited. And remember, this is all about being the example, which means that when you are open to receiving, you are giving the women in your circle permission to do the same.

There are three ways to practice receiving:

1. Take a turn to share, and don't always go first or last
2. Participate in any hugs, massage, or self-care practices in the circle
3. Ask for support when you need it, such as needing a ride or childcare one night

This is not something that comes easily. It's vulnerable to open yourself up to receive. Being able to receive, especially as the leader or facilitator, is a practice. Breathe, relax, and be easy on yourself. You are always learning how to embody receiving as a student.

These three elements, being the example, co-creating, and receiving, create more engagement in your circles because you are leading through participation. Like the old saying goes, "monkey see, monkey do." You can't ask women to do something that you are not willing to do yourself.

BE THE EXAMPLE AND EMBODY FEMININE LEADERSHIP

Being the example of Feminine Leadership is what creates the glue within the circle and has women come back for more. There are also ways to harness your own creativity to create juicy topics, make your circles fun, and increase engagement.

Create Engagement Through Your Creativity

"Let inspiration lead you wherever it wants. For most of history people just made things, and they didn't make such a big freaking deal out of it. Don't worry about being original. Just be authentic."
~ Elizabeth Gilbert

Are you afraid that your circle content won't be good enough? Are you feeling like you don't know where to start when it comes to creating your circle content?

When it comes to coming up with a topic and circle outline, remember KISS: keep it simple, sweetheart. Seriously, less is more. Talk less and don't lecture. You don't need to be a teacher or guru-- just be yourself. Likewise, strip down your outline so there are less activities to "do"

THE ART OF LEADING CIRCLE

and more time to just be. The focus should always be on connection. The more women connect, the more they will be engaged and the more value they will get.

One simple way to put this into practice is to make sure that they are speaking more than you. 80-90% of the circle should be the women talking, not you.

I have a specific process for selecting a topic for circle that feels relevant, juicy, and engaging: I find a problem that either I myself have been experiencing, or I see my friends experiencing. The circle then becomes a solution for that problem.

Pick a core area of life. Some examples could be health, relationships, money, spirituality, sisterhood, or creativity. Which one feels most alive for you or your friends? Let's use relationships as an example.

With regard to relationships, what's the problem you or your friends are experiencing? Let's say the common theme is finding your soulmate. So, you could title the circle: "Women's Circle on Manifesting Love."

One example of your outline could be:

Opening
Group Share
Movement
Paired Share/Activity
Closing

Next, create three to five questions, like the following:

What would your ideal soulmate relationship look like?

CREATE ENGAGEMENT THROUGH YOUR CREATIVITY

What is your biggest fear around calling in your soulmate?
What worked and didn't work about your current or last relationship?

These are great examples of questions you can use during shares and activities, such as in the Puja Style Circle Share.

See how simple and easy it can be? Don't you think this would be a juicy circle that women would get value from?

And, imagine if you didn't need to spend so much time and energy coming up with the content, and instead could just focus on gathering the women and showing up to lead. Sistership Circle provides monthly circle outlines that have powerful rituals and activities, in addition to hot group share questions, that engage women to come back month after month.

Check out the Resource Section to become a Sistership Circle Licensed facilitator to get access to our circle outlines and other resources and tools, saving you the time and effort of coming up with one for every circle.

Whether it is our outline or one you made on your own, it's important that you add three components to increase your engagement:

Fun! Yes, circle can be deep, serious, and intentional, and should always be a safe and sacred space. But it can simultaneously include lots of laughs and fun. Keeping this balance allows women to move out of contraction and resistance and into receptivity and expansion. Dance is one of the most powerful tools to bring more fun into your circle.

THE ART OF LEADING CIRCLE

Play. Think about how children play, without embarrassment or thinking too hard about it. How can you bring the women's natural child-like innocence alive in circle? The answer is, through imagination, curiosity, and games. Bring in childhood toys, make a game out of an activity, and allow them to express their creativity through art.

Celebration. The more women feel significant, like they matter, the more they will want to contribute and engage with the circle. Have women celebrate themselves and one another to bring the energy up, so they viscerally *feel* the new model of women supporting women.

9

Follow the Flow as the Wise Woman

"Be still like a mountain, and flow like a great river."
~ Lao Tse Tung

Earlier, we discussed two powerful feminine leader archetypes: the Mother, who helps women feel seen, heard, and valued, and the Priestess, an energetic tool to embody to create sacred space.

In order to tune into the energy flow of the circle, you can activate another archetype: the Wise Woman, who acts as our guide for tapping into intuition. Remember that archetypes are energies that reside within all of us, regardless of age, life experience, and personality. We carry these energies within our collective unconsciousness. The first

THE ART OF LEADING CIRCLE

thing you need to know about intuition is simply that you have it. You need to *feel* this and know that it is true. Your intuition is deep inside of you. It's part of who you are as the Wise Woman.

Let's move through a meditation to connect with your Wise Woman. You are welcome to read the meditation and then practice it, but you could also record yourself reading the words below and play the recording for yourself as you move through the practice.

Wise Woman Archetype Meditation

> Close your eyes. Take a deep breath in and send that breath down to your navel. Place both hands gently below your navel and continue to breathe in and out of your belly button. Feel your capacity expanding with the breath.
>
> In this space resides your Wise Woman. Tune into that part of yourself that is ancient and all knowing. The Wise Woman is in your gut and also in your heart. She always knows what's best for you and what's in the highest good of all. There is a reason for the phrase "a woman's intuition." It's because that intuition is part of who we are as women. It is inherent in our DNA. We have a biological instinct to tap into the needs of others. As mothers, we are constantly tapping into what our child or infant needs. As women, we do the same with those around us. Whether you have children or not, you have a woman's intuition. You have the ability to feel into spaces, to feel into energy, to feel into people's fields. You know what to do.
>
> Ask the Wise Woman, in this moment, "Wise Woman, what do I need to know right now?" And then listen.

FOLLOW THE FLOW AS THE WISE WOMAN

Trust whatever message you just received. And then open your eyes.

The Wise Woman is tapped in. She has honed her intuition-- and that's really what your job is, to practice trusting your intuition. Practice following it and really tuning in to your body. Your intuition is not in your head. It's not what you "should" do. It's not fear based. It's not logical. It comes from a feeling deep inside your body.

For example, when you feel a contraction in your body, your heart beating fast, your muscles getting tight, your blood getting constricted. That's your intuition telling you something through your body. Just the same, when you feel really excited, that's your intuition telling you something through your body. It's important to trust yourself and start to feel what's happening in your own body to become present to what your body is saying.

In order to start trusting your intuition as a facilitator, you need to first forgive yourself for all the times when you did not trust your intuition and went against yourself, because holding onto those experiences creates a belief of self-doubt. Let that belief go: today is a new day. Becoming a circle facilitator is a new beginning, a time for you to start noticing and paying attention to your intuition by embodying the Wise Woman.

Cultivating presence through stillness and silence will also help you tap into this archetype. It's not about you having all the answers or saying the perfect thing. Silence is important. Remember, as a space holder, the Wise Woman doesn't talk a lot in circle. She sits back and holds the space. When she knows that there is something that needs to shift and something needs to be said, sometimes she doesn't say it right away. She simply listens for it, and so embodying this archetype is really about observation: observing your body sensations, observing

THE ART OF LEADING CIRCLE

your thoughts, and observing the space-- what's going on, what people are saying, what people are doing, and what their bodily reactions are.

There are two main tools to help you tune into the space.

First, do **check-ins**. Ask everyone to say one word to describe how they're feeling; that way, you can gauge the group. Use this tool throughout the circle, so you can become present to any red flags that arise and respond appropriately.

Second, do a **body scan**. Check in with your own body from head to toe and see if you are experiencing any tightness or tension. Are you a little bit off or sad or upset? Chances are that might be in the space as well. Are you feeling super excited and really light? That might be in the space, too.

From here, you can adjust and make sure that you're able to flow with and match the energy that's present. If you are feeling really excited and have really high energy, but you've got people who are in a more tender, vulnerable place, you don't want to step over what they're experiencing. This ability to sense what's present in circle and flow with it is the heart of intuition.

Cultivating the ability to tune in and use your intuition will also help you, as a facilitator, identify when it's time to make an adjustment or deviate from what's on your agenda, which is a crucial skill to have when leading circle.

Outline or Intuition?

"Intuition is really a sudden immersion of the soul into the universal current of life, where the histories of all people are connected, and we are able to know everything, because it's all written there." ~ Paulo Coelho

FOLLOW THE FLOW AS THE WISE WOMAN

Earlier sections of this book are dedicated to helping you prepare for circle, establish your structure, and create your outline. But you also must be able to identify when that outline isn't quite a match, isn't actually serving what's in the space, and make adjustments as necessary. This is when using your intuition comes into play, and you can tune into your Wise Woman to help you do just that.

I'll share a specific example to help illustrate. I was co-leading a one-day event and right in the middle of setting up the group for the peak activity of the day, an old man entered the room, yelling at everyone about the cars that were illegally parked in the parking garage. My co-leader and a participant took him outside to calm him down, but the women were obviously shaken by the experience, so I gathered everyone into a circle to go around and share what was coming up for them.

> So I asked the question: Why did this happen and what lessons can we get from this experience?

You can only imagine how attached I was to doing the peak activity we'd been setting up. It was the best part of the event! But when I tapped into my intuition, my Wise Woman said we needed to scrap the peak activity and instead process and decompress from the unexpected incident. So I asked the question: Why did this happen and what lessons can we get from this experience? Women were crying and it took an hour to unpack everything. And funnily enough, the intention of our peak activity was very similar in nature to what actually occurred, so we actually delivered on the intention without doing the prescribed activity.

THE ART OF LEADING CIRCLE

There are three main indicators that you need to change your outline: an outside disruption, an emotional breakdown or overwhelming feelings, and an energetic mismatch.

1. Disruption in the space:

When the man in my earlier example entered what was a safe and sacred space, it threw off the container. If there is a disruption that comes into the space, you want to address that disruption instead of stepping over it. A disruption may not be as dramatic as someone entering from outside, either; anything that disrupts the container of the circle needs to be addressed, including a knock at the door, a phone going off, the temperature in the room being too hot or cold, background noise, people arriving late or leaving early, and side talk. It's important to acknowledge and process a disruption to maintain the integrity of the space and your integrity as a facilitator.

2. Feelings/Emotional breakdown:

Although big feelings are often part of circle, sometimes it might be at the level of a traumatic experience, where a woman is crying or having a major breakdown. It's important to handle this situation thoughtfully: you don't want the whole circle to be about this one woman and her issue, but you don't want to step over it, either. Instead, preface to the entire group the need to pause and create space for this woman in breakdown, but that the group as a whole won't take much more time. Then give the woman a couple more minutes to move through her feelings, and ask what she needs in that moment.

Or, if your Wise Woman says that kind of focus will create too much drama, you can say something like, "You know what, I am witnessing you in your pain and I can feel your sadness. We need to move on and

FOLLOW THE FLOW AS THE WISE WOMAN

I know it may take something for you to pull yourself back. Can you sit with these feelings and not try to suppress or push them away? And then if it's still there for you after circle, we can process more." You can then buddy her up with someone after the circle to support her if it feels like it is pushing your boundaries.

Whenever possible, draw a connection between what's happening for that particular woman and what's happening for everyone else, so that the experience becomes a lesson for the group and everyone gets value from holding space for her. For example, you could say, "Can everyone take a deep breath and send her some love? We all know what it is like to feel heartbroken and so let's witness her with compassion." Also, make sure that you do a check-in with the group after deviating from the outline to handle an emotional breakdown. Ask everyone to share one word of how they are feeling, or one word of encouragement to that woman.

You may also feel like a deer in headlights, as though you don't know how to handle the situation because the emotions feel too intense. There are really only three things you need to know to handle any situation, no matter how intense it may be:

- **Don't try to fix or coach.** She doesn't need advice or a solution. Take a deep breath and don't do anything for her but hold space and witness.

- **Be okay with messing up.** Forgive yourself, unpack it later to get the lessons, and move on.

- **Empathize**. Put yourself in her shoes. Simply listen to her and repeat back what you hear, so that she feels seen.

3. Energetic mismatch.

What if it seems like everyone is falling asleep, or there is an energetic lull and the group feels sluggish? That means it's time to do a "state change." Tony Robbins is a master at this. Have the women get up and move or do something to shift their energy.

With each of these indicators telling you to move away from your outline, the key is for you to stop, take a breath, and tune into your Wise Woman. If you don't know what to do, ask her: "What is really going to serve the highest good of all?" That might mean asking the circle directly: "How do you ladies want to effectively deal with this?" This is a great example of co-creative feminine leadership, when you come up with a solution together.

Featured Facilitator: Kerstin Weibull Lunberg

This was the second day of a two-day leadership training at our venue with horses in the countryside outside Stockholm. The team consisted of five women, all eager to develop their leadership skills, with three of them training to become facilitators in their own ALIVE horse-assisted program.

The first day had been just amazing. We were all connecting well in the team and with the horses, opening up to giving and receiving and creating a safe space for learning. At the end of the day, we all went to bed filled with a good team feeling, connected to our emotions, and with lots of things to reflect on.

When the team showed up for breakfast the next morning, I could feel a shift in the team energy. The light energy we all left with the previous evening had turned into more edgy energy and I could sense that the team was split into two groups.

FOLLOW THE FLOW AS THE WISE WOMAN

I was planning to take the team a step further together and I had prepared my favorite exercises with horses for that day.

After breakfast, we all went down to the riding arena to meet the herd of horses who were already waiting for us and "stitch together" our circle. As we entered the arena, one of the horses raised her head, pierced her ears, and snorted loudly before she took off, bringing all the other horses in a wild gallop around us.

The team of women got really scared. I quickly held them back, telling all of the women to stay close to me, as two of them headed for the door in a panic.

We were standing there, close together holding hands, and I could sense a mixture of fear and curiosity in the group of women. I asked them to ground their feet in the sand and to take a deep breath, and we started to breathe slowly together. Taking a deep breath in and out, in and out ...

At this moment, my intuition told me that the herd of horses was responding to this human herd's incongruent energy and now we needed to connect with our hearts to try and get a coherent heart energy in the area.

We were standing and breathing together and after a couple of minutes, we could sense the herd of horses calming down, starting to move at a slower pace. I asked the women to look over their shoulders to observe how the horses slowly started to relax, lowering their heads, and coming to a stop. One of the horses even came up to us, gently puffing one of the women with her mule.

Needless to say, I altered all my planned exercises and unexpected and profound things happened to the team of women going deep and having breakthroughs, but not in the way I originally intended.

What was the learning in this situation? What were the horses trying to tell us?

THE ART OF LEADING CIRCLE

Well, the energy we all bring into a space is always present, and as the facilitator/ leader, you need to be aware of this, trust your intuition, and quickly try to shift it in a favorable direction. It may not be as dramatic as when you are surrounded by horses, but it is still important.

Also, what the horses tried to tell me was that an agenda with lots of exercises is good, but you need to be in the present. You need to check what is really going on right now in this moment within yourself, with the team of people you are with, and also outside of us in the room or in the system around us. Learn how to listen in all directions in the circle.

You need to clear, in the team and within yourself what comes up, so you can really be and stay present and connected with your intuition.

Trust your intuition. It is always available if you are willing to connect.

10

May the Circle be Open but Unbroken

"By the Air that is Her breath
By the Fire of Her bright Spirit
By the Waters of Her womb
By the Earth that is her Body

May the circle be open but unbroken
May the peace (love) of the Goddess
Be ever in your heart
Merry meet
And merry part
And merry meet again."
~ Pagan Circle Song

THE ART OF LEADING CIRCLE

I like to think of the opening and closing rituals of a circle as bookends. They hold the container for magic to happen in the middle. The closing ritual is just as important as the opening. The intention of the closing is for women to feel complete, not left hanging, and also open and excited for the next circle. The intention is also that they bring the basic concepts of circle into their lives, so there is an integration between what happens within circle and "without."

There is one chant for the end of circle, where you say, "May the circle be open but unbroken." That is exactly the feeling you want to create at the end. A memorable circle experience will leave women feeling like the circle connection is still there when they leave: unbroken.

When planning the circle outline, remember that if you go deep, you need to bring the energy back up before you end. If you go deep and leave the women there in the dark underbelly, they may feel overwhelmed by emotion, raw, and unable to process on their own. So before you do the final closing ceremony, make sure to have some activity focused on the light.

Let's revisit my earlier example of the circle called "Women's Circle on Manifesting Love." If your group question was "What is your biggest fear around calling in your soulmate?" you'll want to bring the group up at the end with a question focused on the light, such as "What would your ideal soulmate relationship look like?" After they are feeling more positive and upbeat, you close the circle out.

The closing ceremony should include three things: connection, takeaways, and a closing ritual.

MAY THE CIRCLE BE OPEN BUT UNBROKEN

Create connection by either holding hands or standing in a circle together.

Clarify some of the take-aways by having each woman share her highlight from the circle so they are present to the value.

Have a closing ritual to formally end sacred circle time (this can be blowing out the candle, a chant, or the ringing of a bell).

With all of these tools, guidelines, and techniques helping you lead authentic circles that truly emphasize connection between women, you've got all you need to effectively lead a powerful circle. Do you feel more confident knowing what to do, who you need to be, and how to handle tricky situations?

The next step is to announce to the world that your circle is open!

DEAR SISTER

IF YOU FEEL OVERWHELMED
LIKE YOU CAN'T HANDLE IT
KNOW THAT YOU ARE BRAVER
THAN YOU THINK
AND STRONGER THAN YOU KNOW.
YOU'VE GOT THIS.

LOVE, YOUR CIRCLE

Part Two: How to Start and Fill Circles

Leading circle is one thing. Calling in the women to sit in circle with you is another. Starting and filling your circle is all about clarity and confidence. Marketing is the main obstacle women face when stepping into their leadership. They may have incredible facilitation skills, but are either scared to put themselves out there, don't feel like they know enough women, or are just naturally a nurturer instead of an activator. If this sounds like you and you want to know the secret, here it is: it's less about *who* you know, and more about the energy you are putting out there.

As an activator, I've never had a problem attracting women to my events, workshops, programs and circles. I have been leading events, workshops, circles and retreats for over a decade now, and I'm known for creating magical spaces with transformational experiences. I've taken groups to Peru, hosted launch events from London to Mumbai, held three-day events on a ship, and have facilitated dozens of circles around the world and in my living room. I've grown an international organization and helped hundreds of women on their journey as sacred transformational facilitators. This is my sweet spot. When I actually look at what I am doing, it is less about my outreach, and more about my energetics.

I'm going to take you through a five step process to start and fill your circle that includes both the energetics (who you are being) and the outreach (what actions you need to take).

THE ART OF LEADING CIRCLE

1. Clarify: Know exactly *why* you are leading circle so you magnetize like-minded women and inspire them with your vision.

2. Envision: Set your intention so you can manifest with ease and grace.

3. Commit: Get clear on your date, venue, pricing, and timing, so the universe knows exactly how to respond to your envisioned intention.

4. Share: Get the word out by knowing exactly what to write on your event page and best practices for circle promotion.

5. Prepare: Be prepared with checklists to set up your space and access to my exact templates to do either a full or new moon circle.

We'll start by clarifying the *why* so you can call in the women who energetically resonate with the intention of your circle.

Clarify Your Why to Lead

"The flower doesn't dream of the bee. It blossoms and the bee comes."
~ Mark Nepo

Earlier in the book, I used the analogy of the feminine as a flower to illustrate how, if you want to be a powerful circle leader, it's not about what you are DOING in the circle, it's about who you are BEING in your essence as a feminine leader. To get in touch with your essence, start with your *desire* and allow that to inspire you to be radiant and magnetic.

Think of the women coming to your circle like bees coming to drink the nectar of circle, which is the desire. This nectar is what inspires them to join.

When I put on my first gathering, I had no idea what I was doing. I didn't have any circle or priestess training. But what I did have was a

THE ART OF LEADING CIRCLE

deep desire for connection. I had just moved back to my hometown of San Diego from New York and didn't have any like-minded women in my life.

I kept thinking about a luncheon I had attended in New York. It was a simple event for women to connect and network, and I remember thinking to myself, "I want to do something like that!" And so I did. My "selfish" desire to connect with like-minded women inspired me and turned on my power. My essence then was able to show through my actions. This is the first step.

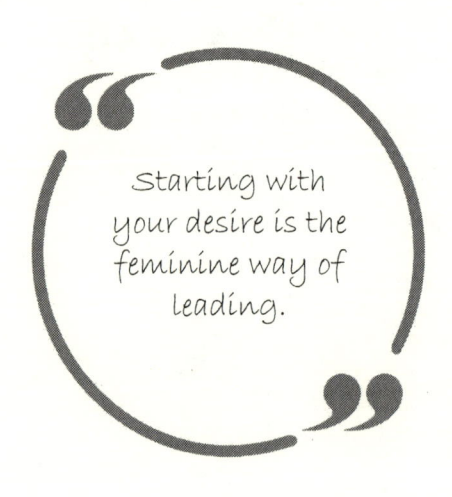

> *Starting with your desire is the feminine way of leading.*

But here's the thing: as women, we have been disconnected from our desires. We've been conditioned to be the selfless martyr, always putting others first. Starting with your desire is the feminine way of leading. It's the solution you've been looking for. Think about it: the more turned on you are, the more tapped into your pleasure, the more exciting you are to be around. The more magnetic you become!

If you are focused on your desires, a few things start to unfold. First, you are modeling to other women what it looks like to not only *have* desires but to also **go after** them. Second, you are taking the pressure off of yourself to immediately fill your circle, because it's not actually about them, it's about you! If it's about *your* desire, then it doesn't matter if only one woman shows up-- you're fulfilling your desire regardless of how full your circle is. Third, you are taking all the pressure off yourself to perform, teach, or serve.

CLARIFY YOUR WHY TO LEAD

Like we've discussed, leading circle is not about being a guru who has all the answers and knows all the right things to say. Leading circle is about holding space for an intention. When you are focused on that desire and invite women into that space, magic unfolds. Imagine leading a circle that fills you up with so much joy and excitement that you can't wait to do it again. If you feel that way, others will too.

Your desire is also called your "Why to Lead." It's what brought you to this book in the first place: something about circle pulls at your heart and soul, just like when I first started for a "selfish" reason to have like-minded women in my life, to find a place to belong. On a soul level, there was something else calling me that I couldn't quite describe, a desire to go deeper within myself. Here's the thing: There is no right or wrong desire. And it doesn't matter if it is your heart's desire or your soul's.

Allow yourself to feel into and name *something* that you desire. Tap into it. Allow it to inspire you. Allow it to burn like a blazing sacred flame so it lights you up. What has made me so successful is that I am connected with this sacred flame. I'm lit up by this work. My passion is contagious. Women can feel it: when I share my WHY, they want to be part of it.

The more connected you are with your big WHY that stokes your sacred fire within, the more inspirational and magnetic you are to those who are aligned with that WHY. This is essential to leading (and speaking) with passion, conviction, and charisma.

For the sake of the following exercise, make this WHY personal and about *you*, not about empowering and helping other women, because then the focus is off of you and onto them.

THE ART OF LEADING CIRCLE

Why circle? What has it done for YOU?

Journal on the following prompts to spark that sacred flame:

>Imagine the first time you sat in circle.

>How did you feel? What did you experience?

>What has healed within you? How has circle transformed you?

>Connect with your wise woman in your womb space.

>Why has your soul called in circle? What does your Wise Woman whisper to you?

>What is the #1 thing you are most passionate about when it comes to circle?

When you share your why, you will talk with such conviction, strength, and passion, that people listening to you are touched, moved, and inspired to take action. How enthralled are those listeners? Do they have goosebumps? Do they believe you?

Your desire matters. Don't listen to the voice that wants you to feel like you don't belong, like there's something different about you, like your community somehow won't accept you if you put this work out there. Don't let anyone or anything lead you to believe that you can't do this.

At Sistership Circle, we have a list of thousands of women out there looking for a circle in their local community, and no women to lead them yet. Women are out there waiting for you. Even if you live in the middle of the woods, they will come out of the woodwork. I've seen it happen.

CLARIFY YOUR WHY TO LEAD

Once you have a clear WHY, it's time to envision the circle.

Featured Facilitator: Dr. Judith "Jai" Belton

The awakening of my true self was a powerful journey home. My path allowed me to leave behind the systems and institutions which influenced a separation of my culture, mind, body, and spirit. Circle integrates my past, the connection with my future, and the full embodiment of my feminine leadership. My suffering as a woman of color is entrenched deep within our country's history and conditioning. I thought I could never move into a state of wholeness. I have felt isolated, having navigated difficult, racially tense power dynamics and microaggressions. This made me always go above and beyond, yet unsure of my own power.

I struggled with finding my flow in leadership because of the programming I received from childhood and extending well into adulthood. My opportunities in education and employment have come with Eurocentric systems and standards. When I began facilitating Sistership Circle circles, I started to realize how disconnected I was. I positioned myself to protect me with all the emotional armor I could muster because there really was not a safe place for women of color to show up. We don't fit the traditional perception of the flower child circle participant, which is another fallacy of the Eurocentric model. I found that I needed to grieve the losses of my ancestors and address the generational trauma's impact. Circle brought all of this to the surface.

This clearly became my vision to hold sacred space for women of color to be seen, heard, and valued by someone who has experienced the world as they have. When we are aligned with our purpose and vision, our deeper needs, such as a sense of belonging, being connected, and doing the kind of work that stimulates creativity is fulfilled. I once held hurt for my ancestors, for the lack of awareness that systems still define and confine us, and for the thought of producing further generational trauma from unhealed wounds. The clearer I become on what I am to manifest, the lessening of the confinement becomes present.

THE ART OF LEADING CIRCLE

The reconnection and embracing of who I am has permitted me to step into a leadership position that creates sacred and safe places for women of color to feel accepted for who they are and not what society tells them to be.

For me, being a Sistership Circle Facilitator is not about the act of circle, it is about giving myself permission to embrace my love for it and stand in my truth as a woman of color who feels rooted in who she is. This is my vision and I am committed to assisting as many women of color reach this place. This is not about wearing certain clothes or having a specific "look," but being adorned with a balance of feminine and masculine energies. I take on the charge for us, women of color, to give ourselves permission to connect with our divine feminine leadership through the creation and acceptance of a standard of our own.

Envision Your Intention

I've shared this before and I'm going to share this again because it truly is the secret sauce.

The secret to manifesting women to your circle is INTENTION.

I set an intention before I do anything because this is what puts everything into motion. It's the north star, your compass. When you set your intention and then let go of the way in which you fulfill that intention, you are guaranteed to create magical experiences in everything you do.

To help you create a powerful intention, I want to share my step by step process so you can use it for yourself, too.

Leading circle is 90% energetics, 10% structure.

THE ART OF LEADING CIRCLE

Who you are BEING as a leader, embodying the words that come out of your mouth, is the most important thing. Congruency in your thoughts, words, and actions is key. So, to make sure you have direction and align your BEING with your DOING, you need to set an intention.

I'll give you an example of the 4 questions I ask myself when I set an intention.

Before we get into the specific 4 questions, first I have to define my WHY to lead: I lead circle because of a selfish desire to feel a sense of belonging and deep connection with other women, as well as step into co-creative leadership so we all rise up together.

This is my overarching theme for all the circles I lead.

One example of an intention for my circle is:

"To activate your feminine wisdom, power, and presence."

Here are the 4 questions I use to set an intention:
- What do I want to leave women with or have them experience?
- How will I know this is happening?
- What do I need to embody to have this happen?
- What do I personally want to receive from this experience?

1. What do I want to leave women with or have them experience?

I want women to feel connected to their sense of power and feel connected to one another. I want them to have insights and awareness coming from their inner wisdom. I want them to be present to what gets in the way and bust through it.

ENVISION YOUR INTENTION

2. How will I know this is happening?

This is key. This is how you can actually picture it in your mind's eye and make it a reality. Examples of how you might know it is happening are engagement, active participation, speaking up, and/or tears.

3. What do I need to embody to have this happen?

This comes back to who you are BEING. Grace and ease as the queen, presence as the high priestess, unconditional love as the mother. Decide who you must embody to bring the experience to life.

4. What do I personally want to receive from this experience?

Bring yourself in so you are fully connected and present and rooted in your desire. What DO you want out of circle? Is it connection, confirmation, empowerment, more energy?

> Write your intention down. You can use the playsheet in the Startup Kit.

Write your intention down. You can use the playsheet in the Startup Kit. This intention is then sent out into the collective unconsciousness of women like a smoke signal.

Next, see it in your mind's eye. Visualize it. Meditate on it. Feel it in your body.

Now you may find that women start to come to you, or hear about the gathering without you speaking to them. It's because their soul in the

THE ART OF LEADING CIRCLE

collective unconsciousness got the message and resonated with it and they are seeking you out.

Notice that we are talking about your intention in the section around starting and filling your circle, because you want to do this first before you even put the word out there in marketing and promoting your circle. You want to stay present to your intention every day from the moment you make your circle public to the moment you sit down and ring the bell to start.

Next you have to commit, which is a requirement for them to say yes once they tap into your intention.

Featured Facilitator: Sharlene Belusevic

Before I started leading women's circles, I had a dream. This dream stemmed from a longing in my heart and soul, a yearning for feminine connection and friendships, and a desperate need to find a tribe I belonged to and could call my own.

The seed for envisioning women in my circle was well and truly planted as I saw the vision of myself surrounded by women who, like me, craved a space to heal, grow, and transform.

That seed has since grown and blossomed into the most amazing sisterhood and consistently filled circles. The initial vision bloomed into reality in a way that went so beautifully far and beyond those very first dreamy, heart desired moments.

For me, the first and greatest step toward envisioning the women in my circles began with listening to, witnessing, and acknowledging a calling and vision from deep within. This was my seed – a seed from the Goddess planted in my soul, and as with any seed, for it to grow into its fullest potential, it required the right environment and nutrition.

ENVISION YOUR INTENTION

It all began with that desire and I knew the next part was to do the inner work knowing full well that it WAS the nutrition. It wouldn't matter what action I took if there was no seeing and believing it was all possible on the inside.

So, I got to work. I regularly sat with my eyes closed and tuned into my heart and connected to my womb space. I pictured in my mind's eye the vision of me leading circles. I saw myself in my circle space, leading a circle with 20 women present.

I felt in my body and heart how amazing it was. I imagined the energy in the room, what the women were saying, how they felt when they arrived, and how they felt when they left. I allowed myself to see and feel all the magic and the positive changes that occurred as a result of all those women coming to circle.

I did this regularly, every time I thought about my circle and before and after taking any action toward putting my circle out there. It wasn't long - literally only two months or so - before I had 20 women coming to my circle!

This was confirmation for me that calling women into circle is an inside job. It starts with our desire, then our intention, and from there, it's up to us to regularly tune in to that and feed it with the energy of possibility until it becomes a reality. It was through regularly tending to the vision in my heart and soul, combined with the grace of the Goddess, that allowed the outward manifestation of women attending my circles.

And if this is possible for me, it is definitely possible for you, sister! So, get envisioning those women because they are waiting for you and your circle.

Commit with a Declaration

"Whatever you can do, or dream you can, begin it.
Boldness has genius, power, and magic in it!"
~ Goethe

Making a declaration to officially commit to the circle is the most challenging part for many women who are afraid of putting their circle out there. I hear all the time a whole list of reasons why they can't commit yet: it's not the right time, they don't have a venue, they have too many other commitments, or they're just not ready.

The truth is, however, that you may never actually be ready. It's like having a baby: you will never actually be prepared, no matter how many classes you take, until the baby has arrived and you are learning

THE ART OF LEADING CIRCLE

by trial and error how to nurse and change a diaper. Day by day you learn how to be a parent.

Same with circle. While you have no clue how it's going to turn out, feminine leadership is about learning how to trust and co-create with a power higher than yourself. So your declaration happens first, including the date, time, and price of your circle. Then you put it out there. The universe responds to definitive clarity. These details may change by necessity, and that's okay too. The universe will still respond to the commitment you are making.

Notice I didn't say the venue. Why? Because the venue always shows up. We're going to cover this more in a future chapter. For now, specify your date, time, and price.

The final thing to get clear on is whether you will lead solo or in partnership. Here's what I recommend: It is beautiful when women co-lead together. It is part of the foundation of Sistership Circle. And, there is a caveat to having a "partner" to lead your circles with. That caveat is that the Sister Wound can easily surface and destroy your circles if you do not have clearly defined agreements and expectations in place with your partner. It's happened to me, and I've seen it happen to many other women: you use a partnership as a crutch because you don't believe that you can do it on your own, and so the partnership is not built on a sustainable foundation.

So instead of going all in with one woman as your circle partner, I recommend "dating" different facilitators by co-leading with various women during different monthly gatherings.

Remember, you do not have to co-lead. This is just an option if you would like some support during your first circle or first few circles.

COMMIT WITH A DECLARATION

Some of the benefits to having a partner are that you don't have to do it alone and that you get to have fun meeting and connecting with other leaders. You also can see who you resonate with the most and try it out first, before making a larger commitment to fully partner with someone. This also helps you reach more women, because each leader has her own network and you are getting introduced to more circle participants that way.

This is why, in our "How to Lead Circle" program at Sistership Circle, you get to practice co-leading one of the circle calls with another sister, to get experience in this area so you know how to create partnership and feel confident in approaching potential co-facilitators.

14

Fill Your Circle Through the Art of Manifestation and Sharing

"The universe doesn't hear what you are saying.
It only feels the vibration of what you are offering."
~ Abraham-Hicks

I've never had a problem filling my circles. Want to know my secret? Here are seven of my energetic tricks to manifesting more women to your circle:

1. It's all in your intention.

THE ART OF LEADING CIRCLE

Everything I do starts with an intention. The clearer I am, the more I manifest, which means being *very* specific. One of the biggest mistakes I see women make is to say "I want more women at my circle!" Well, how many is "more"? They might respond, "10 to 12." That's not specific enough. What's the *one* number you can clearly articulate to the universe? The universe won't know how to respond to vague intentions or confusion around your intention.

2. Tune into the current energy of the circle.

If you are already running a circle, then it already has an energy field around it. It has a vibration that certain types of women are being drawn to. If you can tune in and feel the energy that's already there, you can call in more women to that specific vibration. In order to do this, stop taking it personally if someone says no, and start to see that they just aren't a match (for now). Focus on this energy and don't get distracted by those who are not aligned.

3. Visualize a full circle.

After tuning into the current energy of your circle, focus on that circle expanding. I sit down in meditation, usually in the actual space where I hold my circles, and I visualize what it looks like for that space to be full. I may even put out 12 cushions, if I want 12 women, and then close my eyes and imagine them sitting there with me. The Startup Kit has a link to my visualization audio to help you with this process.

4. Meditate and see who comes to mind.

After I do the visualization in Step 3, I will ask the universe, out loud, who is supposed to be there. I may even draw some goddess cards to help initiate this process. It's amazing what faces or names come to

FILL YOUR CIRCLE

me. And it's even more amazing what happens after that: one woman who I invited to circle was shocked because she was also in meditation to call in a sister circle. This is the power of manifestation, when we tune into the collective energy field and see who's just waiting to be pulled in.

I also always, always, always ask women to bring a friend or refer women they know. The sisterhood extends beyond your mind's eye. It is inclusive. It is diverse. Allow women to bring their friends, who then bring their friends. Create a space of non-judgment and openness and see who is curious to attend.

5. Be who you want to attract.

The circle's energy field is essentially your energy field: the circle is a reflection of you. Whatever energy you are putting out there is what's coming back to you. This means that if you are in scarcity mode, saying things like "Everyone's such a flake in my city," then you will attract a bunch of flakes. Write down some of the qualities within yourself that you want to attract more of and focus on being that person.

6. Express gratitude for women who are already showing up.

Sometimes when we want more of something, we forget what we already have. Can you focus both on the gratitude of who is already showing up as well as your longing and desire for more? Not only that, can you express your appreciation and joy for each woman who is already there? Let her know how much she means to you. Appreciation appreciates.

THE ART OF LEADING CIRCLE

7. Start a conversation.

Finally, while I would say 90% of manifestation occurs on an energetic vibrational level, you still need to take action. Create a heartfelt invitation to the woman who came to you in that meditation. Remain open, when you are out and about, to meeting new women who you can strike up a conversation with and invite to circle. Let women know that you are holding a circle and ask them to share it with their friends, especially the ones who are already showing up.

Here are two actions to take with an example of each for you to use.

Step 1: Take a deep breath and go onto Facebook to write a post letting the world know that you are starting a circle.

Sample post for monthly circle gathering:

Calling all goddesses! Are you looking to connect with a sisterhood where the conversations go deep and we support each other's brilliance? If so, come join us for a Full Moon Circle for ritual, movement, meditation, sharing and activation. [Include the link to the Event page]

Step 2: Send out at least 6 personal invitations via email, text, or Facebook private message.

Sample message:

Hi [name],

I have felt the call to bring together some women for a sacred circle experience. This stems from a longing I have to go deeper with women and truly support each other's growth and expansion. You keep coming up for me. I feel a connection, like we are on the same page. If this

FILL YOUR CIRCLE

is something that you've been wanting to call in too, I'd love to share with you what I am creating and see if you want to be part of it.

Love,
[your name]

Step 3: Repeat! Keep posting and keep thinking of new women. Go to networking events. Ask friends for recommendations of women who would want to sit in circle.

Prepare Your Sacred Space

"If I had eight hours to chop down a tree, I'd spend six sharpening my axe."
~ Abraham Lincoln

You've put it out there and made the invitations. You have RSVPs and some women have officially registered. Circle is happening!

Even if no one has confirmed yet, show up and hold the circle anyway. You want to show the universe that you are serious about this, even if it's just a circle of one (you).

The final step before starting your circle is in the preparation. Go through the checklists, set up your space, and review your outline. It can be easy to get caught up in all the marketing and leave everything to the last minute so you are rushing around in a panic the hour before your circle starts. But the more relaxed you are walking into your circle,

THE ART OF LEADING CIRCLE

the more likely the women are to actually show up. When you are in chaos, it will energetically affect the circle. Women will mirror that chaos and feel overwhelmed, so they will bail last minute.

The key to eliminating that last minute stress is to do all of your prep the day before. Carve 2-3 hours out of your day to go over your outline, pack up your supplies, and tune into your intention.

I want to share with you all that I do to prep, so you can get started without any prior experience.

> *You are here to model authenticity so that you give women permission to show up just as they are.*

The first and most important thing is to let go of perfection. If you forget something, it's not a big deal. If you don't have your outline memorized, it's going to be fine. Remember, circle is about showing up exactly as you are. You are not a guru. You are here to model authenticity so that you give women permission to show up just as they are.

No one will know if you mess up and skip a section of your outline. No one will know if you forget an altar item or play the wrong song. Women aren't coming to circle for any of that. They are coming to be in a safe space to share and connect and be in sisterhood. When you let go of the bells and whistles and get right down to the essence of circle, you actually just need an empty room with some cushions or chairs to sit on, a candle in the middle to signify the spiritual center of the circle, an intention, and a few question prompts.

PREPARE YOUR SACRED SPACE

You absolutely have permission to just show up, even if the room is not "Instagram worthy." And, I want to share with you some tips and tricks to turn a white-walled room into a magical temple space for circle. Over time, you can collect more items and objects to add to your circle box. But when you are first getting started, let go of the pressure and just have fun with it.

Let's start with set up.

Entrance

When women enter the space, you want to do something to invoke the sacredness of what they're going to experience. I suggest smudging and/or anointing.

Smudging is a ritual to cleanse and purify a woman before she enters the space. You can use sage, palo santo, or another cleansing herb that has significant meaning to you.

Anointing is using essential oils to bless the woman before she enters the space. You can look up the various spiritual meanings of oils and pick one that matches the intention of the circle.

Some oils to consider are:
- Frankincense: The Oil of Truth
- Lavender: The Oil of Communication
- Bergamot: The Oil of Self Acceptance
- Geranium: The Oil of Love & Trust
- Wild Orange: The Oil of Abundance
- Clary Sage: The Oil of Clarity & Vision
- Myrrh: The Oil of Mother Earth
- Sandalwood: The Oil of Sacred Devotion

THE ART OF LEADING CIRCLE

You can also use rose water to anoint, which signifies unconditional love. Do some research to find oils or waters that resonate with you and your intention. You can find our list in the Startup Kit.

Environment

Low lighting or candle light creates a soft ambience that invites the sacred. Using an oil diffuser with the oil you are also using to anoint can add to the experience. I also suggest playing some music softly in the background to create a mood.

Seating

Place chairs or cushions in a circle. I would recommend either all chairs or all cushions so everyone is equal. If you are circling in someone's home, I do *not* recommend using any couches, as it affects the mood. Individual chairs or cushions are best.

Altar or Centerpiece

In the middle of the circle, you can have a circle mandala towel (you can find the link to these online in the Startup Kit) or even use a scarf to designate the center altar. The reason we have a center altar is to signify the spiritual center of the circle. Place a candle at the very center to represent that sacred flame.

You can also decorate the altar with flowers, candles, crystals, and other sacred and meaningful objects. Placing a Oracle Card Deck (or a few) within reach gives women a tool to connect with their intention.

PREPARE YOUR SACRED SPACE

Other Decor

First of all, don't get caught up in the decor. Don't let this be a reason not to start your circle. Keep it simple: you can hang meaningful artwork on the walls, or drape fabric of bright colors to add to the atmosphere. You could also bring in plants or flowers to add beauty to the room.

Food

I believe a powerful component of circle is breaking bread together, so I always have a potluck before we sit down to circle. A potluck is when everyone brings a dish to share, which allows each woman to contribute. If you have food, make sure you have thought ahead and brought or asked other women to bring plates, silverware, cups, napkins, and designated trash cans.

Miscellaneous

Don't forget to bring a timer, bell, or chime to call time, a music player and speakers, and pens and paper.

I recommend getting a big plastic bin to designate as your circle box. Put everything in that bin, so you don't have to hunt for separate elements each time you're getting ready for circle. Keep everything organized in one place.

And just like that, you are ready for circle!

THE ART OF LEADING CIRCLE

You know how to lead it now, so the key is in showing up and trusting: trusting yourself, trusting the women, and trusting the medicine of the circle.

You've got this. I believe in you.

Get that first circle under your belt, and commit to keep going and growing your circle.

Featured Facilitator: Jo-Maitera Hall

> "E kore au e ngaro, he kākano i ruia mai i Rangiātea."
> ("I will never be lost, for I am a seed sown in Rangiātea.")

Over the few years that I have been facilitating circles here in Aotearoa, New Zealand, each and every time I am guided by my intuition. From the time I make the decision to offer a circle, the preparation commences. I intuitively call in my sisters and how many I see in attendance. I am intuitively guided to set in place all the fine-tuning details for the day ahead.

Within the circle, we are in our body, our heart space. Our hearts are open and our presence enables each and every Sister to share within a sacred container, to be heard and acknowledged, to be honored. Simultaneously, each Sister has the intuitive and collective presence of honoring and holding space for each and every Sister in circle. We do this energetically, with love and with the reassurance that we each belong here in our circle and we all are safe.

As the facilitator, I conduct the circle with my intentions based on our circle outline. However, at times, this will change. Why? When? How? To be honest, I can never predict any given circle's process on any given day. This isn't up to me. Sure, I can arrive with intention and I can arrive with a circle outline but this won't necessarily mean that our time together will run predictably. In fact, at any given time this can

PREPARE YOUR SACRED SPACE

flip immensely and when this occurs, it is by force of nature and it will be for the better good of all involved. For example, one day I arrived in circle with my laptop. I tend to have printed outlines, but this day I didn't. My computer would not connect and I could not access the outline! I thought, "OMG! I can't even commence this let alone share all the exercises with the Sisters!" I got frazzled! Then I stopped to breathe, connect, and use my intuition. I didn't need the outline. Nobody knew I didn't have it and they sat in circle and trusted me to lead circle. I trusted my intuition. The circle was perfect using an intuitively guided process.

At times I have a circle outline. I may sit in the presence of circle and contemplate if this feels right. If moving on to the next part of my outline aligns with today's circle and where we are at this time. Sometimes the answer is no. Either the shift is too far from the current evolved energetic space where we have arrived, or it simply doesn't intuitively align with today, with the circle, or with my instincts. So, it changes. We delve deeper into discussion as needed. Sisters will be able to have more time to share rather than move on and either avoid the possibility or the opportunity of this process. It creates deeper, more meaningful presentations of opportunities with our circle to share and this is the beauty of being in circle.

So, remember to use your own intuition whenever you facilitate and lead circle. If venues are altered at the last hour or attendees arrive with unexpected Sisters as means of support or to share our circle, technology fails you, or whatever other challenges you feel you are faced with, just remember that these challenges are presented for a reason, in all good timing. It's for you to intuitively seek answers from within, as you are already intuitively able to be guided within circle and conduct your circle just as I have been led to, through the use of intuition, love, and the guidance of my ancestors.

Getting Started FAQs

*"Do the uncomfortable. Become comfortable with these acts.
Prove to yourself that your limiting beliefs die a quick death
if you will simply do what you feel uncomfortable doing."*
~ Darren Rowse

The previous chapters went over the specific steps you'll be taking to start and grow your circle. In this chapter, I want to answer some frequently asked questions I receive about dates and times, money, and venues.

Date and Time

What day of the week is best to host circle?

Really, it's up to you. Go with the day that you prefer or is best for your schedule. There will always be women who can't make it. Stand in your desire and you'll attract the right women. When you start trying to please others, you'll attract more difficulty.

Personally, I prefer Monday evening for a regular circle and Thursday evening for a gathering.

Evening or daytime?

Again, this depends on your preference and availability. Usually, everyone can make it in the evening. You could do 6 - 9 p.m. on a weekday, or an early morning circle from 8 - 10 a.m. Or a brunch circle on a weekend from 10 - 1 p.m. Again, there will always be women who can't make it, but if you stand in your desire, you'll call in the right women for the circle.

What time specifically?

You know the answer by now: what do you prefer? Here at Sistership Circle, we recommend hosting potluck from 6:30 - 7 p.m. and holding circle from 7 - 9 p.m.

To potluck or not to potluck?

The benefit of potluck is that everyone gets to connect and get their chattiness out before they drop into deeper sacred circle space. They also get to arrive on time and have something to eat. I believe breaking bread is an essential part of any gathering.

However, having food may not be conducive to the venue. If you decide not to do potluck, be sure to ask women to arrive 15 minutes before your intended start time, so that you have everyone in the room ready to go on time.

GETTING STARTED FAQS

Also, I highly recommend discouraging alcohol from being served. It can create an unsafe environment or may make some women feel unwelcome. This is actually one of the agreements in my circles.

How much time should I give myself for promotion?

Usually, we start to promote our circles 2-4 weeks in advance. Three weeks is a good standard amount of promotion time. The majority of attendees don't register for an event until the week of (and usually the day before). If people RSVP on a Facebook event, make sure you give them reminders, because they tend to forget. Asking for a formal RSVP or registration on a website is always best to get commitment.

> If you spend all your energy people-pleasing and trying to accommodate everyone, the energy disperses and what you're trying to build simply doesn't happen.

Did you notice a theme here around your preference? Remember: your desire matters. The more focused you are, the clearer you are, the more magnetic the energy of the space you will hold. If you spend all your energy people-pleasing and trying to accommodate everyone, the energy disperses and what you're trying to build simply doesn't happen.

Once, I tried getting a bunch of women's opinions on when we should meet. The answers were all over the place and no one seemed to want to commit. As soon as I asked myself what would work best for myself (Monday evenings), and committed, everyone started to sign up. I learned a very important lesson that day: what I want works the best for me, and will attract those who are most aligned with me.

THE ART OF LEADING CIRCLE

Another common question at this point is whether or not to charge for your circle, especially if it's your first one. Although we'll go over this in detail in the Circle Business Model section, I want to address it here as well.

Money

To charge or not to charge? This is typically the dilemma I see most often for most women's first circle.

Many women believe that sisterhood should not be a commodity and that circles should be free. I disagree. If you are putting time and effort into organizing a circle, expending energy by holding the container and providing a valuable experience, then there should be an exchange of energy, whether that's in the form of monetary payment or a barter. Remember, your time is also a commodity and you must value it.

Here are three distinctions to make for yourself:

1. You are providing an opportunity for women to learn valuable skills they can use to create sisterhood in their lives.

2. You are providing a service to the community.

3. You are holding the space for a transformational experience, much like a personal development workshop, just labeled as a circle.

This does not mean, however, that you need to start charging for your circles right away if you aren't comfortable doing so. My suggestion is to find your comfort zone and threshold level first, and then gradually

GETTING STARTED FAQS

push that further out to where you want to be based on your income goals.

For example: let's say you want to make $500 a month and you are charging $15 per person. That means you need 33 women at your circle to reach your goal. Realistically, you will be getting 15-20 women to attend on average, so you'll want to gradually raise the cost of the circle to $20.

There are 3 different options to explore when looking at charging money for your circle.

The first option is a free circle. If you have never led a circle before, the key is getting your feet wet and practicing to gain confidence, which may mean that a free circle feels best for you. You may want to invite your friends, letting them know you are leading for the first time and would like their feedback in exchange. Notice that there is still an energetic exchange-- their feedback-- for your time, effort, energy, and the experience.

The second option is a donation-based circle. If the circle is donation-based, make that clear on all of your marketing and give a suggested amount. Have a basket available at the door when women walk in. Chances are, they will not leave a donation until afterwards, so when you are closing your circle, let women know that this was a donation-based event. If you need to cover the cost of the venue, let the women know what that cost was and how much comes to per person. If that's not the case, use the analogy of tipping your massage therapist when you get a massage or your server when you go to a nice restaurant: if you liked your experience, donate according to how much value you received.

THE ART OF LEADING CIRCLE

The third option is a paid circle. Circle costs can range from $5 - 30 per person. If you compare that to a yoga class, the sweet spot is $11 - 20 per person. I prefer taking pre-registrations for circle because then I get a headcount of how many women are coming, and I also get women who are serious about circle and fully understand and agree to the cost.

The majority of women who have taken our "How to Lead Circle" program feel confident enough from our training to charge. If I charge, I always extend the invitation for 2 - 4 people to attend for free, depending on the size of the gathering. This way I am providing an opportunity for women to attend who can't afford it to still attend. This is my personal choice, and you are not required to do the same thing in your own circle.

You could also choose to create an early bird discount or a 2-for-1 special, which helps get women spreading the word and bringing a friend with them. You could also provide a certain number of scholarships. Discounts and scholarships work towards making your circle available for all women, regardless of socioeconomic class.

When taking payments, here are some options:

1. Become a Sistership Circle Facilitator and don't worry about it!

One of the benefits of becoming a licensed SC Facilitator is that you can host all your circles on our site, which means you never have to worry about creating a website or marketing materials. We do that all for you, plus you get the instant credibility of being associated with a global brand.

GETTING STARTED FAQS

2. Paypal, Eventbrite, Venmo (US), Zelle, Facebook, or Google pay.

There are so many ways to take payment these days. Whichever you choose, simply create a Facebook Event and post the link to the payment page or account.

3. Cash or personal check.

You can decide whether you want to take cash or check in advance or at the door, but remember, the chances of people attending *decrease* when they don't put money down to commit in advance. It's also nice to have this as a last resort for walk-ins to your circle, such as someone who did not RSVP or a circle attendee who decided to bring a friend at the last moment.

The bottom line with taking payment is this: it all comes down to your sense of self-confidence and self-worth. Money will increase over time, the more you lead circle, so there is no reason to stress yourself out trying to figure out whether you should charge and what you should charge. Tune into your Wise Woman and ask her. She knows what is best for you.

> Why is it okay to charge for a yoga class but not a circle?

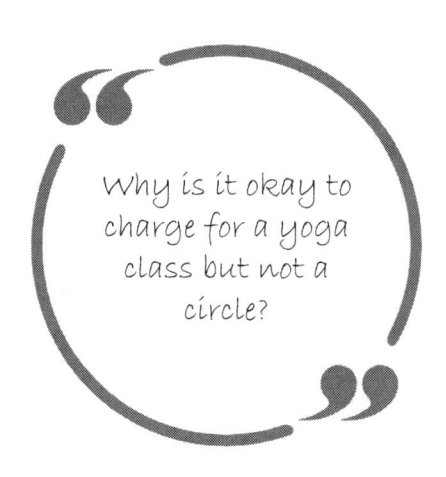

If you're still feeling resistance to charging money for facilitating circle, ask yourself this: Why is it okay to charge for a yoga class but not a circle? Investing in yourself, such as in personal development, this book, coaching, and circle, is important, both to you and to the women in your circle.

THE ART OF LEADING CIRCLE

Venue

Finally, let's talk about selecting a venue. If you feel blocked in this area, know that this is *not* the most important thing. Seriously: you can hold an informal circle anywhere, even in a hotel lobby bar or your living room.

First, identify the block. Is it that you don't want to pay for a venue? You don't know where to go? You've never had to deal with a venue before? Whatever the block is, it is actually making it more difficult for the perfect venue to show up.

Step 1: Surrender the venue to the universe.

As woo-woo as it sounds, this works! The perfect venue will come to you effortlessly as soon as you let go of your attachment to the venue itself and to the belief that it's hard to find.

Try saying: "I surrender to you, God/Goddess/Universe. Please send me the perfect venue for my gathering where women will feel peaceful, connected and alive in their feminine."

Step 2: Ask for recommendations.

Start asking friends for their knowledge and put a post on Facebook asking for recommendations and referrals. Someone's bound to have an idea that resonates with you.

Step 3: Research local venues.

Look into places like local yoga studios, coffee shops, wellness centers, schools, and libraries. In the summer, check for a local park or a bonfire at the beach. All of these are potential venue options for your circle.

GETTING STARTED FAQS

Step 4: Ask a sister to host at her home.

Do you have a friend who has a gorgeous living room space? Ask if she'll host for you in exchange for something. Some people *love* to be the hostess and would graciously say yes! Remember to value her contribution and invite her to participate in the circle for free or give her a gift of some sort.

Here are answers to the most common FAQs about venues:

Which is better: a free venue or a paid venue?

It depends. I personally prefer a free venue hosted at a woman's home, because it creates the atmosphere that I am looking for: comfortable, safe, and homey. The goddess of circles is Hestia, who is the goddess of the hearth. Having circle in front of a fireplace makes it cozy and nurturing.

If you need to find a paid venue, then I suggest charging for the event, either as an upfront fee or donation-based. If you take donations, at the end of the event, calculate how many women there are and how much the venue cost, let the women know that $x per person will cover the cost of the venue, and they will likely donate at least that amount.

Here are some practical suggestions for negotiating with a potential space:

Some venues will do profit sharing with you. The benefit of this is it takes some of the risk off of you when you are first starting. In general, I suggest taking no less than 70% if you choose to do a profit share with the venue.

THE ART OF LEADING CIRCLE

If you do a flat fee, in general, the cost of a venue should be no more than $90 for a 3-hour event (unless you are renting a larger space that holds 100+ people).

Create some exchange. Perhaps the venue staff gets free admission for their guests in exchange for using their venue for free. Or if the location has a cafe, let the venue know you will advertise their cafe and encourage people to purchase food and drinks before the circle.

What are the pros and cons between indoor and outdoor circles?

An outdoor circle is great during the summer, especially if you are doing a fire ceremony. Make sure you have lights, and tell women to bring blankets and pillows. If it is during the day, make sure you have a shade structure and tell women to wear a hat and sunscreen.

The cons of an outdoor circle are unpredictable weather, distractions from other people if you're in a public space, and lighting if your circle is at night. If you do it outdoors, make sure that you create a physical line to delineate the circle boundaries. If you're at the beach, draw a circle large enough as your container with a stick. If at a park, use a rope. Or if nothing else, draw an imaginary line by walking the perimeter of your space. This may sound strange but I swear it works.

I prefer indoor circles, no matter what time of year, because the walls of the room help me hold the container and I don't have to worry about noise, weather, or lighting.

17

Avoid these Common Limited Beliefs

"You may not control all the events that happen to you, but you can decide not to be reduced by them."
~ Maya Angelou

After training hundreds of women how to lead circles, I've seen and heard all the reasons why women think those circles won't fill. But do you know what the biggest block to filling your circle is? It's not having a small network, despite what many believe. It's your limiting beliefs.

When you think that women won't come, they won't. In my experience, there are three most common limited beliefs that get in the way of you filling your circle. Let's examine what they are, and how to avoid them.

THE ART OF LEADING CIRCLE

1. Women in my city are all "flakes."

> *You attract what you put out there.*

You can't possibly say that to me. I live in Southern California, the land of beach bums and non-committals. We are the stereotypical "flakes." But I don't subscribe to that belief. I believe that you attract what you put out there. I let women know the importance of being on time, registering on time, and showing up when they say they will show up. And I rarely have no-shows anymore. The key is in being direct (in a kind, compassionate, and loving way) and letting women know what to expect. Let them know the importance of showing up on time (because you are creating safe, sacred space). They will honor that when they understand.

2. Women in my city don't pay for circle.

Many women subscribe to the belief that circle should be free, but it doesn't have to be. Remember your confidence and self-worth and the value of your time and facilitation. The more you own your value and worth, the easier the money will come and the less resistance you'll find from women.

3. Women are too busy to commit to circle.

Everyone is busy. That's just a fact in the modern world. But we always make time for what we see is important and valuable. We commit to what we want to commit to. So if someone doesn't want to commit, it's just not for them … right now. It may be for them at a later date.

AVOID THESE COMMON LIMITED BELIEFS

Trust that the right women will come together to gather. Trust that the timing is always right.

I know some very busy successful women, and I don't know how many times women have changed their plans to come to my circles. It's because I believe in the value of circle and I convey that value so well that these busy women make the time to come to my circles. You can do the same.

Of course, what and how you share is important. The more you touch, move, and inspire someone to take action, the more likely she is to come to your circle. Focus on sharing the *value* and the *why* more than the details. It's like selling a vacation in Hawaii, not the plane that will get you there. Do you think people care more about the seats and the time of the flight or how they are going to feel once they get there? Share how the women who attend are going to *feel* at your circle.

Here are five important notes to know about sharing:

1. Less is more. Get to the heart of why she should be there, without the fluff.

2. WIIFM. This stands for "What's in it for me?" What will she walk away with? That's what the women who are considering attending want to know. She needs to understand the value and direct benefit she will receive when she comes to circle.

3. Make the invitation personal. Send out a private message instead of just adding women to a Facebook event. Take time to personalize the message for each woman.

THE ART OF LEADING CIRCLE

4. Focus on what makes her special to you. Why do you want to connect with her personally at the circle? Why does her presence matter to you? Let her know she matters.

5. Have a conversation. I have found that if I can talk to someone in person or on the phone, they are far more likely to come than if I just send them a link. This is why I don't do flyers. They are too impersonal and personal connection is very important in effective marketing, in sisterhood, and in circle.

Overcome Overwhelm and Get Unstuck

"Never give up, for that is just the place and time that the tide will turn."
~ Harriet Beecher Stowe

If you're still feeling stuck by limiting beliefs and overwhelmed at the idea of getting started, this chapter is for you.

What I consistently see happen over and over again is women who read books and take courses and still struggle to take the action needed to really start earning money as a circle facilitator.

It's not your fault and you aren't doing anything wrong. The truth is, we accomplish so much more when we are held accountable and feel supported by a circle and a mentor.

THE ART OF LEADING CIRCLE

I can only give you the "how to" in this book. I cannot see who you are, and cannot provide you personalized guidance based on your individual needs. But, we can do that if you joined the "How to Lead Circle Program," our Sistership Circle level 1 certification.

If I look at everything I have been successful at, it's been because I was held accountable and supported by mentors and peers. My results have skyrocketed when I have been in a group container. Why?

Accountability

Left to your own devices, there is a greater chance you will procrastinate and get distracted. When you are held in a group container, you have the structure to keep you focused and on track.

Support/cheerleading

There is nothing like having other women cheering you on, telling you you've got this and that you're doing great, to inspire you to keep going. This helps you believe in yourself when you get into a swirl of self-doubt.

Collective intention

There is something magical that happens in a group; when everyone holds each other's intentions, they happen.

Blindspots

You can't see what you can't see. But with peer and mentor support, your blind spots can be pointed out to you to help you move through.

OVERCOME OVERWHELM AND GET UNSTUCK

This is all offered in the How to Lead Circle Program, along with much more, including access to our global platform, branding, monthly circle outlines, and marketing materials. We have a very high success rate: over 75% of women start their first circle before they graduate and an additional 10-15% shortly thereafter. So if you want to get out of the overwhelm and frustration of getting stuck, I highly recommend joining us for the full-length certification program.

More importantly, you will never be alone again.

By becoming a Sistership Circle Facilitator, you have that support for the lifetime of being a circle facilitator. You get the resources, tools, curriculums, peer support, mentorship, and accountability to keep the momentum going and grow your circle business. You get to be part of a movement, contributing to something so much greater than yourself.

DEAR SISTER

THE CIRCLE REFLECTS YOUR LIGHT
THE CIRCLE REFLECTS YOUR SHADOW
THE CIRCLE REFLECTS
ALL PARTS OF YOU
WHAT PARTS ARE YOU
WILLING TO SEE?

LOVE, YOUR CIRCLE

Part Three: Growing Your Circle

Once you've started your first circle, you've overcome one of the biggest hurdles-- actually getting started. Most women fail at leading circles simply because they never follow through on getting that first circle under their belt, or they do the first one and then stop.

In this section, I'm going to cover some important topics so that you can grow your circle community. This is the place for you to get all the information to keep growing your circles after you successfully lead the first one.

We'll go over:

- Our Sistership Circle business model, so that you can increase your impact and your income leading circles.

- How to keep the circle healthy over time with conflict resolution and conscious completion.

- A powerful strategy to keep attracting more women to your circles.

- What's going to burn you out and how to avoid it.

- The 4 stages of community and how to effectively build an active community.

THE ART OF LEADING CIRCLE

- The inner work you need to focus on in order to keep growing as a feminine leader.

This section is packed full with deep content, so keep referring back to it as a resource as you move forward in being a circle facilitator.

Keep the Momentum Going

*"Success doesn't come from what you do occasionally,
but comes from what you do consistently."*
~ Marie Forleo

Over the years, I've watched women as they successfully start their first circle, get so excited, and then a few months later, they are nowhere to be found. They seemingly get distracted by life, and before long their first circle is a distant memory. What happens in this scenario? Is it shiny object syndrome? Do they not have what it takes to succeed? Neither of those excuses is true. If you're afraid this will be you, that you won't be able to follow through and keep hosting your circles, I have a secret for you. There's only one way to keep the momentum going.

Consistency.

THE ART OF LEADING CIRCLE

Once you have your first circle, you need to *continue* to commit to holding a monthly circle gathering every month for the next 6 months. Book it out in your calendar. It can be every full or new moon, the first Thursday of the month every month, whatever works for you. Remember to focus on your own needs instead of trying to figure out how to please and accommodate others.

Commit to consistency, no matter how many women show up each month. Consistency is the key to your success.

Being committed and consistent improves your facilitation skills, attracts more women to your circle, and helps you build confidence. You'll improve your facilitation skills simply from the number of hours you are putting in. You will attract more women to your circles because the women in your circles will start sharing it with their friends and inviting them to join. You'll build confidence as you start to use the tools more regularly and feel like you've got a handle on this circle leadership thing.

When I dug in to see why the women were falling off after their first or second circle, I found the missing piece: they were not declaring their circles or setting any goals. They resisted making a plan of action and implementing that plan. This plan of action, the masculine structure and container, is what creates consistency.

Here's a step by step plan to create 6 monthly gatherings, the number I believe is needed to get going and truly build momentum.

Step 1: Declare when the circles will be for the next 6 months, and put them in your calendar so nothing else can take precedent. Start telling the women when your circle is going to be held so you have

KEEP THE MOMENTUM GOING

accountability. Make this a big loud commitment and start sharing and promoting your circle.

Step 2: Say no to any invitations that come up during your circle time! You will inevitably get invited to a party, or have "something come up" during that time you booked out in advance for your circle. Say no! It is important that you take your scheduled circle commitment seriously and not let anything push it to the side or entice you to reschedule. Remember your why and don't allow external things to push aside your circle and the commitment you've made. If you are wishy-washy on your commitment, the other women will be, too. As you know, circle is a mirror. I'll also introduce you to another archetype in Chapter 22 that will help you set those boundaries.

Step 3: Create S.M.A.R.T. goals with milestone markers working backwards from 6 months, then 3 months, then 1 month. S.M.A.R.T. is a goal-setting system which helps you make sure your goals are clear and attainable. The acronym stands for Specific, Measureable, Attainable, Realistic and Timely.

For example:

You state that your goal is to impact 100 women and make $2000 in the next 6 months.

That goal meets some of the criteria right off the bat: it is specific and measurable and has a time-based focus of 6 months.

Let's break it down and see if it's also achievable and realistic.

100 women divided by 6 months is about 17 women per circle on average. Some circles may have more or less, but 17 per circle is the number you want to shoot for.

THE ART OF LEADING CIRCLE

$2000 (your income goal) divided by 100 women is $20 per person per circle. You must decide if you are comfortable charging that amount. If you aren't, then this is the time to revisit your goal. Maybe it needs to be 150 women impacted, so that you can make the same amount of money by charging less per person. Or maybe you amend your financial goal to $1500, making it $15 per attendee for 100 women impacted and making the goal feel achievable and realistic for you.

The goal you make should be a stretch, but not "out of reach" where you are setting yourself up to fail. You want it to be an achievable goal that takes work and dedication to reach, but *is* possible for you.

If the numbers above feel too big or too much, then perhaps for the first 6 months you want to decrease those numbers to 10 women per circle so the total is 60 women impacted with an income goal of $900, which will have you charging $15 each.

Now that you have created your full 6-month goal, it's time to create a 3-month goal inside of that overall one. Let's use the numbers from the BIG goal.

Take the 6-month goal and divide it in half. So, in 3 months, you want to impact 50 women and make $1000.

Do the same for the 1-month goal so you can know exactly what you need to be reaching for every single month. Your 1-month goal would be 17 women and about $334 total.

The most common resistance to setting goals like these is the fear of failing. But what I have found over ten years of experience is the opposite: having specific and measurable goals provides direction and

KEEP THE MOMENTUM GOING

accountability. Ask any successful person, and they will tell you they set goals for themselves.

If you don't reach those goals, it's important to celebrate what you did accomplish, review your framework to see where the gap was, and then reexamine your new goal for the next 6 months. You can use the Goal Setting page in the Startup Kit to track your goals and your progress.

As you continue to hold these monthly gatherings, you will begin to build a reputation for yourself and establish credibility in your community. And as your reputation grows, you'll be able to grow your circles and serve a wider group of women.

Featured Facilitator: Rae Ireland

I've spent a lot of time creating momentum. You may be able to relate. So many projects and ideas come into my mind that sometimes it feels like a tidal wave is moving through me and knocking everything else away, including old projects and ideas.

I caught on to this pattern while I was looking at my old songbook. I flipped through the pages of song notes while thinking about how I still hadn't released my solo album. In fact, completion was far from my focus point. All the songs were basically ready to go and just needed a few final touches, so why was it taking me so long to finish? Why was I so resistant to completing this project?

I began to notice every reason I came up with as a "good excuse" as to why my album still was not released was actually covering the truth. I was terrified about putting my name out there and having my loved ones hear my vulnerable songs about the past few years. I felt like an awkward fraud. I had so many musicians on this album, it wouldn't have been even close to sounding this good without them. I "just"

THE ART OF LEADING CIRCLE

wrote the songs, played a few simple instruments, and sang. That's all. Of course, looking back now I see how silly this was.

I realized I was so wrapped up in myself and my ego that I had forgotten the vision of why I was sharing my music in the first place: I wanted to make people feel, connect deeper to themselves, and know they aren't alone. Oh yeah, there was that sweet spot! I realized I MUST continue to remind myself of this "why" daily to actually be ready to host my album release party. Well, guess what? Only a few months later, I hosted the album release and it was a great success!

This reminds me so much of launching my business and hosting circles. It often happens that I lose the beautiful momentum I started off with. I've learned that this is okay and totally normal. I've also learned the keys to maintaining that momentum with consistency:

1. *Be aware of when you lose your momentum.*

2. *Be kind to yourself and whatever excuses you're using to validate why it's okay to put your goal to the side.*

3. *Understand what you're getting out of not following through with your plans (safety, security, not looking dumb, minimizing risk, etc.).*

4. *Reconnect with your original intention and why you built up momentum in the first place.*

5. *Set yourself up for success with support - a team, coach, tribe, calendars, reminders - try one or do them all.*

6. *The next time you lose momentum again, start over at step two.*

It's a beautiful process and so worth the roller coaster, so you may as well enjoy the ride!

Embrace Collaboration

"Collaboration is multiplication."
~ John Maxwell

Do you want women to keep coming back to your circles AND also have new women attend so that you have consistent growth of your community? I'm going to share something with you that has been integral to the consistent growth of my circles.

But first, I want to share with you the biggest pitfall that will get in the way of your growth: when you try to do it all by yourself.

If you want to grow your circle, increase your impact, and build a community, you need to get out of your own way. You can't be the bottleneck, and you can't be the martyr. As a recovering martyr, I get it. I struggled to trust others and I also didn't want to feel like a burden by asking for help. I wanted to prove myself capable and worthy by taking it all on solo.

But here's the secret to doing all of those things: collaboration.

The more that you embrace collaboration with other leaders, the faster your circle is going to grow. If I look at how I have been able to create sold out circles, fill every single program, and grow an international organization, it is because I have reached out to other leaders to be part of, support, and share my mission.

Of course, the idea of collaborating with other women can bring up so many old wounds and limited beliefs, such as:

"If someone promotes what I'm doing, how will I compensate her?"

"Why would anyone want to promote my circles when they have their own business to worry about?"

"Why would anyone want to be a facilitator at one of my circles for free?"

This all comes back to your mindset and limiting beliefs. Other women have been so excited when I asked them to share on social media or to email their list about what I am doing. I'm going to tell you exactly how I get their support, so that you can do the same.

There are three things that you need to do to have a collaboration partner come on board:

EMBRACE COLLABORATION

1. Inspire with your *why*.

Back in 2013, I went to London to do an event. I didn't know anyone in London, but I started to do some research to find existing community leaders. I went down some rabbit holes on Meetup and Google until I found some spiritual women leaders in London who I felt drawn to. I reached out and asked for a conversation on Skype, where I shared my passion and excitement with them. I shared my belief in the power of collaboration and sisterhood and they said, "Wow, I love what you're doing! How can I support?"

2. Make an ask.

You must make a direct request telling them exactly how to support you. The clearer you are, the greater the chance of them helping you. So I give a specific action and a deadline like this: "I would love for you to send out an email to your list between these dates. Let me know if that would work for you."

3. Give them an incentive.

Your incentive doesn't have to be monetary. We think sometimes that we have to pay someone to help us. Instead, consider giving them free tickets to attend your circle and bring friends so they can be generous to their community. You can also offer an exchange, where you will promote their next event to your list.

And sometimes they just want to help and be of service because they believe in the mission of what you're doing and are willing to help you for free. But it is still good karma and courtesy to offer an incentive for their help first.

THE ART OF LEADING CIRCLE

4. Make it easy to share.

Always give them exactly what you want them to share: the written Facebook posts, the written email to copy and paste. I have a file of "Marketing Copy" that I send to them with the disclosure that they can use this word for word or make it their own. Most leaders in the community are very busy and have a lot going on. The last thing that they're able to do is take their energy away from their business to write their own email for and about you, especially if they don't know you very well yet. When you are able to do that for them, chances are better that they'll send it out.

Here are three of the easiest ways to collaborate:

1. Trade or exchange

The most common way to collaborate is the idea of an even exchange. When you ask people to share your event on their social media, send out an email, feature you on their podcast, have you on their Facebook Live, or speak at their networking event, offer to do the same for them for a future event.

2. Have her be a guest facilitator

Another way that you can have collaboration is by inviting someone to facilitate part of your circle. By inviting her to be part of your circle, you're giving her access to your network and also giving her the value and healing and transformation of circle. Some of the ways they could be part of the circle are by having them lead the opening meditation, a movement activity, or a connection exercise.

EMBRACE COLLABORATION

3. Give her valuable connections.

One of the best ways to provide value and get people to support you is by being a connector. Ask her what she's up to and what support she needs. Then, go through the Rolodex in your mind of who you can connect this person with, whether that is a client referral, another collaborator she should meet, the best place to host events, or your favorite hair stylist. You are providing massive value, so she will want to return the favor.

As you can see, there are different ways you can bring people in to feel like they're part of what you're doing, and in return, they share your event with their community. The whole point is that you are getting exposure to someone else's network and collaborating with them to get it.

And finally, we can't forget about networking. You've got to get out there and meet more women if you want to grow your network. Go to other circles, events, parties, anything to meet collaboration partners or circle participants.

When you go to a networking event, it's less about how many business cards you come home with and more about the relationships you initiate. Set an intention to connect with 3 quality women at every event. Take your time and drop in if you feel a resonant vibe. Then follow up! Get a lunch date on the calendar and play the connection game by asking, "Who are 5 people you think I should know?" and then get a warm introduction to that person.

But make sure that you are developing authentic relationships, and not just courting a woman because she can do something for you. You will build your community by being known in the larger community as someone who is generous, the real deal, a connector, and someone other people want to know.

Of course, this is a lot of work. It's in service to a big why, and something that you're passionate about and committed to, but that doesn't mean it won't affect you. It's important to take care of yourself first and foremost, so we're going to address one of the biggest reasons women stop doing circle work, and how to address that reason.

Featured Facilitator: Kristin Jensen

In 2018, while coaching with Tanya in the Mastery of Circle program, I held a launch party for my new circle business and first course. I structured the event around Reclaiming Our Sovereignty in the areas of the seven chakras. I reached out to several local feminine leaders and had six of them facilitate a 10-minute section on one chakra each, with me facilitating the seventh section. It worked out pretty well – about 30 women attended. All of the facilitators were happy to participate – they each had space at a table to gather contact information from women who wanted to work with them further, and I made sure to give them all glowing introductions. Most brought one or two women to the event, some more, some none.

It was my first attempt at putting on an event and bringing in collaborators to assist with facilitation and promotion. The next time I put on an event with co-facilitators, I will design the agenda so each facilitator has much more time and the event will focus just on 2-3 topics. Seven topics were a lot to fit into a four-hour event! I stressed about how much time each person took, several women went over their allotted time, and our event ended late. I was under a tight timeframe getting it off the ground, and the agreements I made with each facilitator around their promotional activities were verbal. I will give myself more time to put on the next event, and create signed agreements for all collaborators and the venue with clear expectations around them promoting my event to their communities.

EMBRACE COLLABORATION

My launch party did open the way for me to develop an ongoing collaborative relationship with one of the facilitators, Emily, a sex educator, who gives frequent workshops and sees private clients. In early 2019, she came as a pro bono guest to my monthly circle to present on sensuality. When I ran my flagship circle program in summer 2019, Reclaiming Your Voice, I hired Emily to come work with the participants as a special guest expert. One of the women in my course became her private client.

This winter, another friend and I co-hosted a workshop for Emily around female pleasure and orgasm – a wild success, with 45-50 women in attendance. I brought the community and my friend provided her home. My friend and I both promoted Emily's workshop and we each brought several women from our respective communities and social circles. In exchange, Emily gave us each a complimentary session, and she took the time to introduce me and promote my circle and my courses at the beginning of her workshop.

Emily is a master at incentivizing collaborators and hosts – her model is to give a private session to each host who brings at least eight women to her workshops, plus she gives a gift to the woman who hosts the event at her home. I've learned much from watching her. We have both benefited from our collaborative relationship and have become close friends in the process.

21

Avoid Burnout

"Burnout is what happens when you try to avoid being human for too long."
~ Michael Gungor

We're going to go over a checklist of different sources of burnout and what to do about it. The first thing to know is that burnout is not only experienced as exhaustion. Burnout can be caused by anything in the space that takes you out of your power. If there is any point in your journey when you feel like giving up, that you are just done leading circle, that means something is hijacking your power.

Anything mentally or physically exhausting, draining, sucking, burdening, distracting, hijacking, disrupting, causing distress or anxiety-- all of that falls into the category of potentially causing burnout. Let's go through this list to help you dig underneath the

THE ART OF LEADING CIRCLE

physical symptom to get to the source of what's burning you out. It is critical as a leader that your practice self-are on all levels: physical, emotional, and spiritual.

PROBLEM: Something is bothering you and instead of addressing it, you are avoiding, denying, or ignoring it.

SOLUTION: Try to identify it by asking the question: What feels like it is draining and sucking your energy? Focus on specific things until you find what is causing the issue.

PROBLEM: You're not feeling supported by or you are feeling burdened by the group. You may be feeling like "too much to bear."

SOLUTION: Trust and let go. It's not your job to fix or heal anyone. Don't go into default "over-nurturing feminine mode" to the point that you are over-giving. Instead, focus on holding the container and providing the right space and energy.

PROBLEM: You are feeling triggered by a participant.

SOLUTION: Feel your emotions fully, process any withholds, and take responsibility for everything, even if it feels "unspiritual" or immature. You are human and you will have judgments come up. Instead of bypassing because it feels unspiritual to get angry or frustrated with someone, call yourself out on it. This is why it is important to have a mentor or be in a training program when you are first leading circles, so that someone can help you take responsibility and move through what you're feeling.

PROBLEM: You indulge in self-criticism and feel like you aren't doing it perfectly.

AVOID BURNOUT

SOLUTION: Focus on why you're doing this work, your personal "why," and the incredible gift you are sharing with the world through circle. Identify and use your support structure to hold you when you doubt yourself and help you clear negativity or old beliefs about yourself. You are going to make mistakes as a facilitator. Again, you are human. But if you beat yourself up, the doubt and worry can lead to burnout and exhaustion. Give yourself room to be human and don't overthink mistakes. Learn from them and move forward.

PROBLEM: You didn't plan ahead and are stressing out on the day of your circle.

SOLUTION: Schedule less on the day of your circle. Prepare as much as possible the days before. Refer back to the suggestions in this book for how to prepare ahead of time and avoid feeling overly stressed on the day of your circle.

PROBLEM: You've been taking too many discounts and not getting paid for your facilitation, which results in resentment.

SOLUTION: Own your value and worth and the sacredness of your role. Start small: if you are leading circle for free, start taking donations. If you are taking donations, start charging a small fee.

PROBLEM: You're trying to do too much and fixing other women's problems during circle.

SOLUTION: Trust the process of circle itself to create the exact space of healing that everyone needs. Practice letting go of being the one who needs to fix everything and everyone. Learn how to receive. Coming from the overbearing sense of "I've got to do something for these women. I've got to make the difference for them" will deplete

THE ART OF LEADING CIRCLE

your energy. The circle itself has the medicine, each woman is carrying her own medicine, and there's nothing that you need to heal, fix, or do.

PROBLEM: You're having trouble managing kids, partner, and other obligations and maintaining balance with leading circle.

SOLUTION: Take a sacred stand for your work and step into your power with self-love and without threatening your loved ones. Ask for support from everyone in balancing it all so that this vital and important part of you can be expressed in the world. You've got to learn how to delegate and have your family step up with their contributions, like cooking dinner and doing chores. If you are doing it all yourself, the laundry, the kids, the work, and the circle, something has to give. It's time to step into the archetype of a Queen. Can you take a stand for yourself and the work you are doing as a circle leader? Can you value yourself and your time and energy? It will be an adjustment if your family is used to you doing 100% of everything all the time. But if you respect yourself and your boundaries, they eventually will too.

PROBLEM: You're doing everything for your circle yourself.

SOLUTION: Activate your Queen energy by asking for help from others with logistics, set up, and clean up. This is not about you carrying the burden all by yourself and carrying the women in circle, but creating a co-creative leadership circle where everyone is a spoke on the wheel. Everyone's a contributor to the wellbeing of the circle.

This is a lot. It's a whole new paradigm. There is a lot of old conditioning in our way and holding onto those old ideals is what burns us out. It's simply unsustainable. When you open up and let people contribute to you, do the deep clearing work to change the limited beliefs that keep

AVOID BURNOUT

you stuck, and let go of holding it all yourself, you step into yourself as a Queen and stay radiant.

Being the Queen is something that we strive for. Becoming that powerful woman who can say no, set boundaries, take care of her own needs, and be a stand for everyone's needs being met is a major shift.

Featured Facilitator: Deborah Harlow

I vividly remember the first Sistership Circle I facilitated. I had checked all the boxes and navigated the process with precision. I approached each piece with a trained eye, as special events were part of my professional background and in my blood as the daughter of a chef. The feedback from the circle was glowing and I felt a spark of joy in me I had not felt in years.

However, I was utterly exhausted by the end of the circle - both physically and emotionally. For the first couple days after circle, I was in a fog and questioned if I could really continue on with a process that asked so much of me (or so I thought). As I approached the next month's circle, I began to feel resistance and when no one signed up or showed up, I felt deep resentment.

I felt that facilitating circle was the missing piece in my life, so how could something that felt so right to me be so challenging to bring together with others?

And in the question was the answer: I was not bringing it together with others. I was approaching the circle as an event. I was good, nay, great at event management, and had over two decades of successful events under my belt, so why couldn't I shift that successful track record into this area?

The weekend after my "failed" second circle I made arrangements to be alone with my thoughts. My hubby and daughter spent time on their own so I could sit with what needed to be acknowledged in me. Circle had shown itself to be the missing

THE ART OF LEADING CIRCLE

piece of my medicine wheel, so I was not going to accept that this was the end of the journey.

I sat in quiet reflection reading through my notes from the How to Lead Circle program. I closed my eyes and remembered the moments I spent in deep connection with my sisters. I danced wildly around my office with music playing loudly. I dropped to my knees in tears as lifetimes of buried hurts burst through flooding every inch of my body.

I didn't know how to receive. I didn't know how to connect. I didn't know how to collaborate. I knew how to fix, create, and control. Life had made damn sure of that. No room for mistakes. No room to trust others. It was no surprise that my first circle transitioned from pure bliss into my second circle as pure devastation.

I went for a walk outside and observed how each piece of nature was sovereign unto themselves all while collaborating together in a sacred dance of synchronous union. I walked back home and sat down to write what needed to come through - my why, my ask for support, my Queen voice.

On this journey, I have come to trust that when I own my Queen voice and stay connected to my why I am able to honor that my role is to experience circle as healing for myself through being the sacred container ... then everything falls into place ... not always as I imagine but always as I need it to.

Stay Radiant as the Queen

Self-care is not self-indulgence. It is self-preservation."
~ Audre Lorde

Learning to embody the Queen archetype will help you stay radiant and not burn out.

Of the archetypes we've looked at so far, the Queen can sometimes be the one who is hardest to embody because of the bad reputation that she's gotten in our society. We think of the Queen and we think of *Alice in Wonderland* and the Queen of Hearts yelling, "Off with her head!" Or, we may think of the ice queen, or the evil queen in *Snow White*. Really, what we think of when we hear the word "queen" is a dominating, bitchy, mean, controlling woman. And so, of course, we shy away from wanting to embody "the queen" because we don't want to be that kind of woman.

THE ART OF LEADING CIRCLE

But here, we're approaching this idea of the Queen not from a hierarchy, but from the concept of circle. What we're talking about is being a good queen, a radiant queen, a woman who is coming from her heart space and serving because she feels like she's so filled up that she is able to keep her head high and serve from her heart outwards to all the people around her. This queen is a sovereign woman.

The word *sovereignty* is so important. Sovereignty is about you owning your domain. Circle is your space that you are taking care of, something that you hold sacred, and you are claiming that role as guardian of the space. This is what the Queen is doing when she sits in circle: she's able to lift everyone's energy up with her own, so that people want to be in her presence.

Take a moment to do the following exercise and see how you can feel yourself embodying the queen, standing in your sovereignty. If possible, try this in your actual circle space.

> Stand up tall. With your arms outstretched, your chest and head up. Say out loud: "I have the right to take up space on this planet." Feel the truth of that statement with every cell of your body.
>
> Hold your arms out as if you are holding the energetic space around you. Say out loud:
>
> "I have the right to lead circle on this planet.
> I have the right to claim my sacred role as a circle facilitator.
> I have the right to take my stand for women's empowerment on this planet at this time."
>
> Speak anything else that comes up. Say it, feel it, mean it: take this opportunity to claim what you are speaking. This is about you saying "Yes. I can do this. I'm claiming this. I'm good at this."

STAY RADIANT AS THE QUEEN

Feel the power of taking up your space as a sovereign queen, a good queen who is fully serving her family, fully serving the women in her community, and fully serving the sisterhood while simultaneously serving herself. Embrace this new sense of sovereignty in your being.

The Queen practices exquisite self care. When we think about self care, many of us think about taking a bubble bath, making sure we're eating healthily and exercising, and so on. We know the "self-care to-do list," but that's not *exquisite* queenly self care. The self-care we're talking about is an inside-out job. It means doing the inner work to get your needs met on an energetic level so that you are radiant.

Your needs are equally as important as anyone else. It's up to you to not only identify your needs on a daily basis, so you don't burn out, but also to ask for support to get those needs met and to set healthy boundaries to prevent self-sacrificing, overgiving, and depletion.

One of the biggest needs of any circle facilitator, to keep her energy up and maintain the well-being of the circle, is to do constant self-clearing. Clearing means making sure that you keep yourself free from negative, burdening thoughts -- the ones that have you spiral down into despair. Begin to notice how much you complain and dwell in negativity.

There is a crucial difference between complaining and clearing. *Complaining* is making the laundry list of everything that's wrong with you, with others, with the world. *Clearing* is taking all those negative thoughts, judgments, and criticisms and letting them go. Clearing is seeing that they -- the thoughts, judgments, and criticisms -- are the problem, not you or anyone else. Clearing is also shifting from negative

THE ART OF LEADING CIRCLE

self-talk to speaking of and to yourself with self-love, acceptance, and appreciation.

For example, say you have a "bad" circle: everyone showed up late or didn't show up at all. You're beating yourself up about it, spiraling down the drain, feeling worse and worse about yourself, telling yourself you're an incapable leader, judging them for their lack of integrity. Resentment and frustration are building. You are the Queen of Hearts, ready to chop off some heads!

At this moment, you can turn things around. Here's how you can embody that sovereign queen who stands in her power and claims her right to be here:

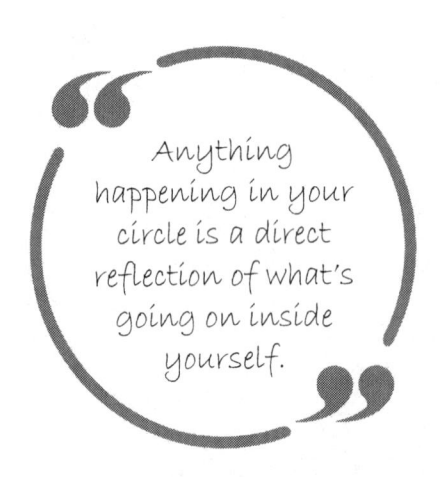

> "Anything happening in your circle is a direct reflection of what's going on inside yourself."

First, take a look at the mirror.

Anything happening in your circle is a direct reflection of what's going on inside yourself. Take responsibility and ask yourself questions like:

What am I *doing*?

Who am I *being*, that these women are showing up late or not showing up at all?

Am I projecting a limited belief that the circle isn't valuable?

Am I saying that I'm not worth it?

Am I saying that this is too much, because I'm too much, and I don't want to be too much?

STAY RADIANT AS THE QUEEN

Second, call it out. Call these things out loud to yourself. For example:

"I'm responsible for my belief that I am too much, and I don't want to be a burden on these women. And because I am afraid of being a burden, they are finding circle to be overwhelming. And I'm going to have a conversation with them where I'm going to own this and resolve to do better. I'm not pointing a finger and demanding that they be on time. Instead, I'll tell them that I've been withholding something that feels vulnerable to share. I'll share with them that I have been feeling like I am a burden, like I'm not good enough as a facilitator, and from that I'm seeing that they aren't valuing circle because I'm not valuing myself. They're not showing up on time or not showing up at all. I've done some digging, I see that this is what's going on, and I'm calling myself out."

Third, call them in.

After you call yourself out, make a rallying cry, calling them back into the circle by saying something like:

"Sisters, I am here tonight humbly calling you all in. What do you need to commit to showing up on time and for us to co-create? What do you need to make this circle so valuable that you wouldn't miss it for the world?"

Can you see how self-clearing is really in service to everyone in the circle? Taking responsibility and clearing yourself clears the energy for the whole group. The heaviness lifts for everyone. Everyone feels light, connected, and inspired by the level of vulnerability and self-respecting responsibility you show. A Queen serves her community with this level of integrity and love.

23

Understand Community Building

"The overall purpose of human communication is - or should be - reconciliation. It should ultimately serve to lower or remove the walls of misunderstanding which unduly separate us human beings, one from another."
~ M. Scott Peck

When women feel like they are part of a community, they will show up month after month and your circles will be full. You need to create the glue, the sticky point that has women come back. Through understanding how to build community, you will create a snowball effect for your circles. Each month, you will find it easier and easier to get women to show up, because it's no longer just about you: they are showing up for each other and the community you all are building.

THE ART OF LEADING CIRCLE

M. Scott Peck, author of the bestselling book *The Road Less Traveled*, wrote another, lesser known book called *A Different Drum*, which has influenced my understanding of communities tremendously. Peck says that every community has to go through four stages in its building process, which I want to share with you here:

Stage 1: Pseudo-community

When women first come to circle, they may have a concept in their head of it being the "best thing ever," so they try to fake it. Everything is rainbows and butterflies. Everyone is super nice to each other, avoiding any and all disagreement or conflict. This is pseudo-community, and the basic pretense is the denial of individual differences. The essential dynamic of pseudo-community is conflict avoidance. This group may appear to be functioning, but everything is happening on the surface level, and the group lacks true intimacy or depth of connection.

Stage 2: Chaos

All of a sudden, the honeymoon stage is over and chaos erupts in the space. This chaos always centers around well-intentioned but misguided attempts to heal and convert. In this second stage, those individual differences that were repressed or denied in the pseudo-community stage are now out in the open, and instead of trying to ignore them, the group is trying to eliminate them. Judgment comes into the space. People are triggered. People want to fix, heal, and convert one another to make everyone and everything return to "normal." Since chaos is unpleasant, it is common for the members of a group in this stage to attack not only each other but also their leader. This is where communities disintegrate and fall apart, unless they move on through chaos to the next stage.

Stage 3: Emptiness

There are only two ways out of chaos. One is into organization—but organization is not community. The only other way is into and through emptying out the barriers. Everyone in the group needs to empty themselves of all their barriers to real communication. This needs to include: expectations and preconceptions; prejudices; ideology, theology, and solutions; and the need to heal, convert, fix, or solve. As the members let go and empty themselves of these barriers, it dawns on everyone that they are seeking comfort in trying to "solve" their differences because it is confronting and challenging to be around others who trigger you or who you judge as less than (or better than) you. It is difficult to leave behind these ideas and barriers, let go of judgment, and stop trying to fix other people's problems, but it is absolutely essential to building a true community of sisters. The group then moves into appreciation and celebration of interpersonal differences, and onto the next stage.

Stage 4: Real Community

When everyone is open and empty, the group enters Real Community. In this final stage, a soft quietness, a kind of peace, descends. An extraordinary amount of healing and converting begins to occur in this stage, now that no one is trying to force healing or conversion. A true community has been born.

What happens next? The group has become a community. Where does it go from there? What, then, is the task of the community?

There is no one answer to those questions. It's primary task may be no more than to simply enjoy that experience and benefit from the healing that accompanies it.

THE ART OF LEADING CIRCLE

Short-term communities are typically ones created during a retreat, 6-12 week circle programs, or any other container with a set end date. This community will have the additional task of ending itself. Somehow there must be closure. The community of people who have come to care for each other deeply needs time to say goodbye. The pain of returning to an everyday world without community needs expression. It is important for short-term communities to give themselves time for ending.

Long-term communities are ones which last for longer than 6 months and have no set end date. Women are in it for the long haul, and again, the task of the community may vary. And while at some point in the future the group may end and need closure, what's more pressing is understanding how to help an individual transition out while the group continues, a process we call "Conscious Completion" which we'll go into more detail in Chapter 28. People will leave and new people will join. It's a natural part of the cycle of communities.

People seek community because they want to belong. And they think that all they have to do to belong is just to find their group of like-minded people, which is why they get so disappointed and start to judge any and all differences within the group at the beginning. So, to bring new women into the existing community, and to create a culture of openness and authenticity, you have to guide women through these 4 stages.

There are three key takeaways from these community-building stages:

1. It's important for you to understand the warning signs of chaos in Stage 2 so that you can move the group to the important emptiness of Stage 3. Chances are, a group will go through chaos more than once. Each time, bring them back to emptiness and then into community.

UNDERSTAND COMMUNITY BUILDING

2. Understand that the task or purpose of the group is to connect, heal, and grow together, and to keep presencing the WHY that we discussed earlier in Chapter 11, or the vision of these gatherings.

3. The more women are connected to the vision and hold it as their own, the more committed they are to working through the chaos when it comes up.

These lessons show that it takes some work to be a skilled facilitator and to build a community, which is why I believe you are providing a service and that you should be compensated. Remember your worth and the value of circle and building community: ultimately, it's truly priceless.

24

Make Money with the Circle Business Model

*"Every time you spend money, you're casting a vote
for the kind of world you want."*
~ Anna Lappe

Whenever I talk about the business of circle, and being able to make money leading circles, there seems to be a huge backlash. So many women out there think that it is terribly wrong of us to bring money into circle. They believe that sisterhood should not be commoditized, that women's circles should be free, and that we're excluding those who can't afford it, making circle a service for the privileged. They claim that by having circles be free, everyone is equal.

THE ART OF LEADING CIRCLE

But not all circles are created equal. Some circles are very potent and transformational. Some are not. Some are more advanced than others. Some have different intentions. The blanket statement that *all* women's circles should be free is simply not true, and I'd like to make my case for the paid ones and why you should absolutely be charging money to lead circles.

In ancient times, priestesses lived and worked in the temples and were taken care of by their community, perhaps not in the form of money, but they got everything they needed taken care of, including food and clothing and adornment-- everything that we now use money to purchase. As a modern-day priestess, why should you provide this service, where women get massive value and transformation, and not be fairly compensated for that like your ancestors were? What this issue really comes down to is you *owning* your value and the value that you're providing by creating, organizing, and holding the space.

As I see it, there are five reasons why you should charge for circle:

Reason 1: Women are getting value.

If a woman goes to circle and leaves feeling filled up, connected, recharged and transformed, then she received value. If a woman goes to circle and a connection comes out of it that she didn't have before, like a new friend, a new client, or a new resource, then she received value. If a woman goes to circle and cries her eyes out, releasing some pent up energy that's been there for a long time, then she received value. If a woman goes to circle and shares a shameful secret that she's told no one before, and she finally feels free, then she received value. If a woman goes to circle and gets a hug after having a terrible day, then she received value.

MAKE MONEY WITH THE CIRCLE BUSINESS MODEL

When a woman gets value, she wants to thank the source. If she goes to a restaurant, it's customary to leave a tip for good service -- the same if she gets a haircut or a massage. Why not make it customary to "tip" the facilitator for rocking a woman's world at circle?

Reason 2: The importance of an exchange in energy.

The facilitator has put in a ton of time and energy to put together this circle. All the effort you put in to gather the women by making phone calls, creating a Facebook event, and sending messages. The time you put in to get there early and set up the space. The time you likely also spends cleaning up afterward. And that's not even counting the energy you put in to create the intention and any activities and then actually holding the space to create an amazing experience.

True, circle facilitators are doing this from their heart because they love the work. They are receiving by giving. However, there is something potent about creating an exchange of energy. To give an offering of your own in exchange for the offering you've received is an honoring of the process; it's an acknowledgement of the time, energy, and effort that went in to create this space for women to come receive what they need. In today's world the most common energy exchange is in the form of money. Taking payment is the honoring of that energy exchange.

> "Imagine for a moment if the wealth of the world shifted into the hands of spiritually-gifted women."

Reason 3: Breaking the cycle of poverty-mindset amongst women.

Imagine for a moment if the wealth of the world shifted into the hands of spiritually-gifted women. What would change? What would become possible? Right now, we live in a world that exchanges energy through forms of currency. Why not empower more women to have more money so we can do more good in the world with it? Money is not evil. There is nothing wrong with having it. We, as women, do not need to be broke. We do not need to be poor to prove that we are spiritual. When we buy into the poverty-mindset, we put ourselves at a disadvantage in the world. We are not serving anyone by being poor, especially ourselves.

To break the cycle, we must start to see the truth about money: it is a form of energy that comes back to you when you give it away. When we hoard it, we live in scarcity. When we hold onto it out of fear of losing it, we are blocking more of it from coming in. What if women considered paying for circle as a tithe, giving it to thank the source for feeding your soul? What if women blessed their money and gave it to show the universe that they are open to receiving more of it in return?

Reason 4: Investing our dollars into a cause in order to see it thrive.

Women have no problem paying for a haircut, a yoga class, or even a drink at the bar, so why not pay a sister for sharing her gift with the world? When we pay for a circle, we are supporting the cause of sisterhood in the world. We are saying, "Yes, I believe in this movement and I want more of it." Just like donating to a non-profit you believe in: we want that cause to thrive. In the case of circle, it's not just about thriving, but surviving.

Reason 5: Supporting a sister's livelihood.

The woman facilitating circle is also trying to make a living. She may have other mouths to feed. She has to put a roof over her head. She may have to take another job that she dislikes to make ends meet.

MAKE MONEY WITH THE CIRCLE BUSINESS MODEL

She's doing whatever it takes. What if her sisters supported her being in her sweet spot as a facilitator? What if, instead of having to spend her energy working another job, she got freed up financially by her community so she could focus on becoming a better facilitator and creating more space to serve more women in the world? Don't we want more empowered women to make the world a better place?

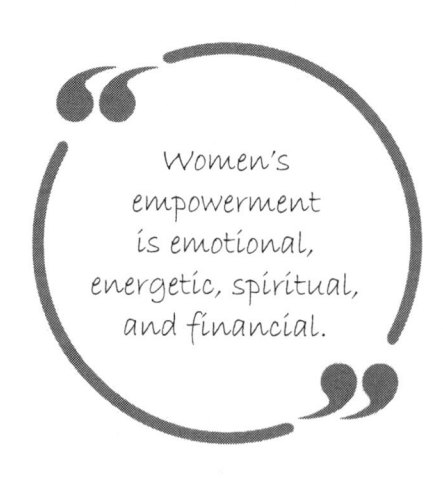

> Women's empowerment is emotional, energetic, spiritual, and financial.

When a woman invests in circle, her investment will come back to her and then some. There is more than enough money to go around. We must break out of the scarcity mindset and live in a world of abundance, where there is enough for everyone to be successful. Women's empowerment is emotional, energetic, spiritual, *and* financial. Let's take care of one another. If circle is about lifting one another up and celebrating each other's brilliance, then let's support each other financially as well. Together, we will change the paradigm, so spiritual women are thriving, creating a new example of what wealth can look like for the next generation.

Sistership Circle Business Model

Truth be told, this is actually my favorite section because of my passion to help you make money doing something you love. Supporting ourselves with work that aligns with our purpose is so fulfilling, and I love seeing how much money Sistership Circle pays our facilitators each month.

THE ART OF LEADING CIRCLE

So let's talk about the official Sistership Circle business model and how to use it. This model is based on the concept of increasing both your income and your impact. We have identified 4 primary stages, and we have created each of our 4 certification levels to help our facilitators reach the next stage.

Stage 1: Hosting consistent monthly circle gatherings.

The intention of the first stage is to impact as many women as possible. The whole point of your monthly gatherings is not necessarily to make money, but to have an open door for more and more women to come in and experience circle. Therefore, your goal for your monthly gatherings is to have 20 to 30 women show up every single month.

This is how you build your circle community, get referrals, and create word-of-mouth marketing. You charge a nominal fee, anywhere from $5 to $25, so that women become used to giving money for circle. They value it, but it's such a low price point that attending is a no brainer. This is also where you can create scholarship and volunteer opportunities for those who cannot pay at all.

Our motto at Sistership Circle is "No Sister Left Behind," and this is how we do that. While we encourage you to charge for your circle, we are not saying that only people of a certain socioeconomic status should be allowed to attend. And by charging money to those who can afford it, you will have the resources to be generous and donate to women in need.

As we talked about earlier, at this stage, you get those six monthly circles going consistently to build your community, so that you get up to 20 to 25 women attending month after month. Having a consistent monthly gathering is the first stage.

MAKE MONEY WITH THE CIRCLE BUSINESS MODEL

We've mentioned in previous chapters how our Sistership Circle Level 1 Facilitators have each started their first circle during the How to Lead Circle Program and are focused on increasing attendance at their monthly circle gatherings while participating in the Facilitator group.

Once you've built momentum and enough interest, usually around the 6 month mark, you'll want to make that leap to Stage 2 to increase your income.

Stage 2: Hosting long-term circle program (8 to 12 weeks in length).

The intention of the second stage is to make a bump in your income.

At Sistership Circle, we provide our Level 2 certified facilitators with three 8-week curriculums called The Awakening Series and a 12-week curriculum called The Experience.

These longer-term programs are where you will start to earn more money leading circles and building community. You'll charge women for attending and committing to those long-term programs, where they go deeper into their transformation, which is an increased value to them.

For an 8 to 12 week program, you can easily charge anywhere from $200 to $500 per woman. Let's do the math: say your price point is $300 for 8 weeks and you have 10 women. That's $3,000 total or $1,500 a month for the life of the 8-week program. That's pretty good supplemental income. If you were to charge $500 to lead 10 women through the 12-week program, that would be $5000 total or almost $1700 per month during the program. You could also lead multiple circle programs at a time and earn more each month.

THE ART OF LEADING CIRCLE

Because this is a big leap, we designed an entire program called the Business of Circle to meet the needs of the women striving to reach Stage 2, giving them the support and accountability to put on a launch event that will draw enough women into a room, along with mentorship to effectively extend the offer for women to invest in their circle program. Our Level 2 certified facilitators then have built enough momentum and have the skills and tools to offer circle programs one after the next.

Once you've established your circle programs, you want to make the leap to stage 3 to increase your influence.

Stage 3: Hosting advanced circles, retreats, workshops, and 1:1 coaching.

The intention of the third stage is to become someone who people want to learn from on a deeper level. You've become a respected community leader. This is where you can start adding on retreats, longer advanced circle programs of six months to a year, one-on-one coaching, and group workshops where you are teaching, not just holding space. You are creating a larger and more varied sphere of influence.

We've designed the Mastery of Circle course to help women develop their first workshop and learn deeper transformational facilitation and coaching skills.

Once you are rocking stage 3, and it's becoming more effortless, many women want to make the leap to ignite the leadership in others.

MAKE MONEY WITH THE CIRCLE BUSINESS MODEL

Stage 4: Become a Sistership Circle trainer.

As you are working this business model, you are an example of what it looks like to be a successful circle leader, so when you reach stage 4, you will have the knowledge and the wisdom to help others do the same. And at Sistership Circle, this is where you can become a trainer and teach other women how to lead circles of their own.

25

Play Your Edge

"The depth of darkness to which you can descend and still live is an exact measure of the height to which you can aspire to reach."
~ Laurens van der Post

I've said this before, but it bears repeating: You are only able to lead a group as deep as you are able and willing to go.

To grow your circles, you need to grow yourself. Remember, the circle is a mirror of you. If you find yourself shrinking back and playing small, then you're probably going to find that your circle won't expand. You're not going to attract more women. But if you are constantly looking at how you can play your edge, how you can grow and stretch yourself, chances are your circle is always going to be growing as well.

The first place you can look at playing your edge is with your vulnerability.

THE ART OF LEADING CIRCLE

What I have found is that women in general feel so uncomfortable being truly seen. They feel uncomfortable revealing themselves. And if you are someone who really struggles with being vulnerable, chances are women are going to feel tentative when they come into your circles. They're not going to feel like it's 100% safe to be fully themselves, because they sense that you are holding back. They might not know to say this as feedback, but energetically and unconsciously, they feel it.

One of the things that you can do to expand and grow your circles is to bring in sensitive topics. And yet this brings up a lot of fear: If I bring in a sensitive topic, do I know how to handle what might come up? Can I effectively hold space for it? Seven of the most sensitive topics are: sex, sisterhood, race, sexual orientation, body image, mother wound, father wound, and trauma. These are typically taboo subjects. Women have experienced wounding, there are hurt feelings, and it can be really challenging for someone to want to go there.

But when you create these transformational experiences, where women say, "Wow, this is the first time I've ever shared that in my life. I feel so much more free and open," they are going deep and are going to recommend your circles.

Being vulnerable is one way that we can grow and expand. It's not just in terms of the number of women who attend, but also the depth of the circle itself.

Now this requires advanced facilitation to take a group through sensitive topic discussions.

Here are seven ways for you to take the group deeper.

1: Develop presence within yourself.

PLAY YOUR EDGE

Presence is one of your most powerful tools as a facilitator because it allows you to be with anything that comes up in the space during circle. One great tool for working on developing presence is *The Presence Process* by Michael Brown, where he takes you through breathwork and 10 weekly exercises to develop your inner presence.

2: Learn how to feel the full spectrum of an emotion, from rage and grief to ecstatic joy.

The more you are able to emote, the more comfortable you're going to feel when emotions come up and are expressed in your space. As you learn to feel and lean into and work through all different emotions, you'll be able to guide those emotions out of others who are dealing with new or difficult ones.

3: Understand the Karpman Drama Triangle.

We teach more about the drama triangle in our certification programs, but on a basic level, the Karpman drama triangle is a power play with three different roles in conflict: a victim, a martyr, and a perpetrator. When you start to understand this triangle, you can identify it and redirect women back into a healthy circle and away from the triangle dynamic.

One reason some women are afraid of coming to circle is because they don't want to relive the drama they experienced in childhood and high school with other girls. They have scars from unhealthy relationships with the mean girls at school or don't truly understand a healthy sisterhood relationship, and they don't know enough about circle to know what the sisterhood bond and community feel like yet.

THE ART OF LEADING CIRCLE

The more you heal your own sister wounds and remove yourself from the Drama Triangle in your relationships the easier for you to navigate this in circle.

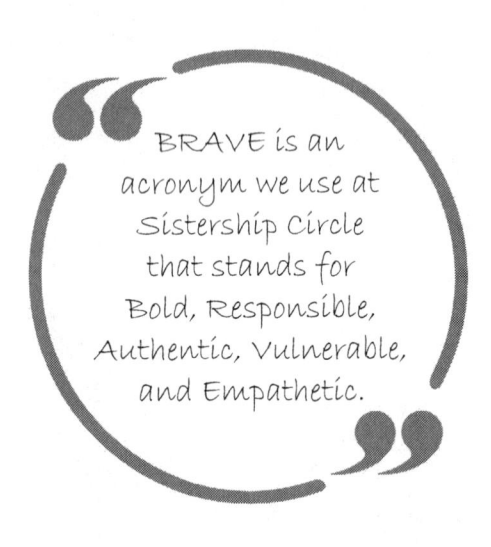

> "BRAVE is an acronym we use at Sistership Circle that stands for Bold, Responsible, Authentic, Vulnerable, and Empathetic."

4: Dig into the places where there is avoidance.

This is what it means to be BRAVE. BRAVE is an acronym we use at Sistership Circle that stands for Bold, Responsible, Authentic, Vulnerable, and Empathetic. You must be willing to be bold and to talk about the things that usually people don't want to talk about. It's about calling out the elephant in the room and being authentic and vulnerable when calling out your own stuff and empathetic to others dealing with theirs.

5: Indulge in honest truth-telling.

This goes along with digging into those places everyone else is avoiding. That is when you are able to speak the truth. Being real and telling the truth can be scary, but it is so refreshing and modeling that behavior helps the women in your circle also embrace their truths and go deeper.

6: Have courageous conversations.

That woman who said that she was going to come and didn't show up: are you willing to call her in? Are you willing to have a conversation with her around integrity and responsibility? It can be hard and scary to have these conversations, but as the facilitator and leader, it is your responsibility to have courageous conversations and call things out when you need to for the highest good of the circle as a whole.

7: Stand for someone who is struggling.

One of the things that we talk about at Sistership Circle is that there is no sister left behind and we always have each other's backs. There is so much mistrust in the world that we tend to avoid getting into other people's stuff so we mind our own business. But what if you were the one who stood up for someone when they were struggling? You want to have everyone's back in your circle. Imagine what that would do for the community.

26

Keep the Circle Healthy

"Peace is not the absence of conflict but the ability to cope with it."
~ Mahatma Gandhi

Women gathering together is truly magical, but it can also bring up a lot of old wounds and triggers. So, let's spend some time talking about conflict resolution and keeping your circle healthy.

There are three things that can cause a crack in the container and make a circle fall apart:

1. Withholds.

A withhold is an un-communicated charge or energy, either positive and negative, that exists between you and another person. When women are holding onto things like judgments, opinions, hurt feelings,

THE ART OF LEADING CIRCLE

and triggers, and they're not speaking about them from fear of rocking the boat, you can feel that in the space. Remember that every circle has an energy and it is your job as the facilitator to be paying attention to that energy and creating shifts as needed. Whenever someone is holding something back and suffering in silence, if they hold onto it for long enough, it's going to drive them away and change the energy and the circle can fall apart.

At Sistership Circle, we have a powerful withhold tool we teach in our certification course and provide our facilitators as a way to teach women to have courageous conversations and empty out judgments. This creates a safe space for someone to share when they are triggered. And the whole point of the withhold tool is to create connection, to bring people back to love and affinity by releasing and letting go of the emotional charge.

2. The group is no longer present to the WHY or the value of circle.

When someone loses sight of the reason they signed up for circle, and they start to think it is no longer worth their time, something else --anything else -- will take precedence over attending. There is a high chance they will then drop out, which cracks the container. When this happens, it can lead other women to think, "What's wrong with the circle? If she's leaving, maybe I should leave," and so on.

It's very easy to forget that circle is the place to get support and be held through it all. They forget why they started attending and they start to diminish the circle's effect in their minds. You can resolve this by constantly speaking to the value of the circle. You can share the why every single time that you start a new circle. At the opening ceremony, share the value of what they're going to get during that circle, and during the closing ceremony, ask them to share the value that they got

KEEP THE CIRCLE HEALTHY

from that day's circle. You can also ask women to share what's opened for them since the last circle. Those testimonials will bring inspiration alive and keep women connected from one circle to the next.

3. Women are not feeling connected.

She feels misunderstood. She got her feelings hurt by another woman. She feels triggered and an old sister wound arises. She feels like an outsider. Any of these things will cause a woman to want to run away. And the more women that run away, the faster that the circle will fall apart.

You must hold the integrity of the container through agreements to create safe space so women feel they can lean in to talk about the vulnerable things that are easier to avoid and sweep under the rug.

What Causes Triggers to Arise

> When a woman gets triggered, her inner child is feeling like she does not belong or she is not significant.

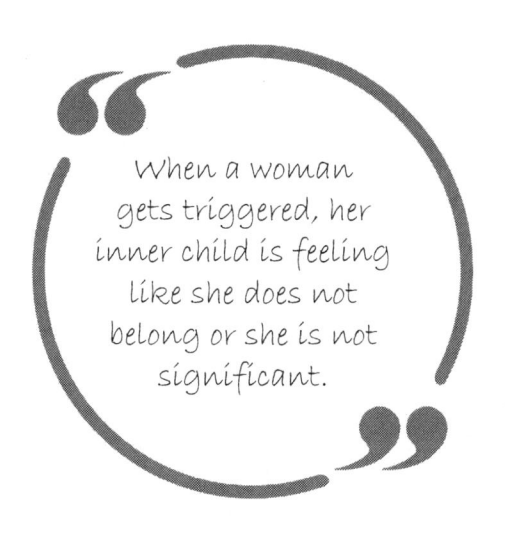

Every child is looking for two things: belonging and significance. When a woman gets triggered, her inner child is feeling like she does not belong or she is not significant. She feels misunderstood, unseen, unheard, and unvalued.

For example, imagine Amy walks into the room and starts giving hugs to everyone except Beth. Beth gets triggered and thinks, "Does Amy not like me?" What did I do?" Amy didn't mean anything by it, but Beth doesn't say anything. The next circle, Beth comes in late. Amy

THE ART OF LEADING CIRCLE

indirectly makes a comment about how annoyed she is when people are late. Beth is even more triggered and feels judged. Her inner child is hurt and feels unseen by Amy. And while this is happening between Amy and Beth, and maybe Amy doesn't even realize that Beth is upset, there is a charge of energy in the entire space. The whole circle is now impacted.

As the facilitator, you don't need to take sides, because no one is right or wrong. Amy is not aware of the impact she's having on Beth, while on the other side Beth is feeling insignificant and like she doesn't belong. Your role is to hold space to help them let go of judgments and get into each other's worlds, so they can come back into affinity and the circle can restore itself. You now need to practice healthy conflict resolution to assist in this process.

Resolving Conflict in Circle

Here is a step by step guide to resolving conflicts that come up during circle:

Set an intention.

I talk about this all the time because it is foundational. Just as you set an intention for your circles, you set an intention for what you want to happen in this conflict resolution, so that all parties feel seen and heard and can come back to love and affinity. Co-create this intention with whoever is involved.

Listen and recreate.

Have each woman share her perspective. Ask the woman who is hurt to go first (let's call her Person A). First, A shares how she is feeling.

KEEP THE CIRCLE HEALTHY

Person B then repeats back word for word what she heard. This is what we call "recreation." When Person B is complete, she asks, "Did I get that right?"

Person A then says yes or no. If she says no, then Person B repeats what she heard again until she gets it right.

When Person A says, "Yes, that is correct," Person B then asks, "Is there anything else?" until Person A is complete.

Then they switch, so both women feel heard.

As the facilitator, you are holding space and playing the meditator to make sure no one starts defending, blaming or judging, and that they are each speaking from the "I" perspective, such as "I felt …" As soon as someone starts to defend herself, it creates more tension because the speaker does not feel heard or validated.

How do you listen without getting triggered or reacting to defend yourself? Take a deep breath and become present to the sensations in your body.

Let's say someone in circle was triggered by you, as the facilitator. It's the same thing: listen and recreate. Empty out the thoughts in your head that you did something wrong. Soften yourself to receive her words and resist the urge to defend yourself.

Get vulnerable.

Only do this once you have fully recreated what was said or done. Have the other woman share what she is feeling and experiencing. Tell her to drop out of the thoughts, which are judgments and stories, and get

221

into her body. This is what allows us to go into a state of vulnerability, which is where our feelings live.

For example, "I'm noticing a really uncomfortable tightness in my chest right now. I feel really sad. I'm wondering if you're sad as well?"

Ask how this could be repaired.

You can ask something like, "What do you need to feel reconnected again? How can we repair this rift in the relationship?" Don't push for resolution. Sometimes space is required. Let go and trust in the process. And if one or all people require space, ask when would be a good time to follow up.

When Circle Goes Sideways

One of the biggest challenges is navigating resistance, or when chaos erupts right in the middle of a circle.

I'll share an example with you. During a three day event, resistance came up right before one of the peak transformational activities[2].

The activity we were about to do was on a sensitive topic around our bodies, specifically around our sexuality as women. Immediately someone said, "I don't want to do this" before I even gave the instructions. I could feel the panic coming up in the room. I felt my whole body go tense and suddenly I wasn't quite sure if I was going to

---

[2] Have you noticed a pattern here? Earlier I shared a similar story in which the peak activity got derailed... That's no coincidence. Know that if you plan to go deep, stuff comes up right beforehand.

KEEP THE CIRCLE HEALTHY

be able to do the activity -- at least not with this panic happening. The circle was going sideways.

Here's a 3-step process you can use any time there's resistance in the space or the circle is getting hijacked and going sideways.

1. Create an open discussion.

As soon as I felt that fear within myself and within the room, I said, "Okay ladies, let's talk about this. Let's have an open discussion."

2. Immediately create space for all their concerns and fears.

In the open discussion, I asked for everyone who had any type of fear or concern around an activity about their bodies and their sexuality, to just speak freely about anything coming up for them.

3. Let go of your attachment to the plan.

If all we were going to do was to have this discussion about their fears and concerns, I had to trust in that. I energetically made myself an open vessel to receive all of the fears and concerns. I was not going to try to resist them. I was not going to try to convince anyone to continue. I wasn't going to try to fix, change, or coach anyone. I simply needed to listen. And in listening, what we noticed as a group was the fears start to dissolve, and all of a sudden, we came to a place where we could feel a palpable shift of energy in the room. I could tell the energy had shifted because I could hear it in the shares and I could also feel it in my body. I was no longer feeling that tightness and constriction anymore.

THE ART OF LEADING CIRCLE

4. Honor their sovereignty.

At that point, I gave everyone a choice. I said, "Here's the activity we're going to do. You can do it, or you can step out of the room and come back in an hour." Everyone had that choice, and I treated everyone with respect, like they were all sovereign queens who did not need to be manipulated, forced, or coerced into doing anything. That permission made it safe, and we were able to move forward with the activity as a group.

I'm going to be real with you, though: this is advanced stuff and not easy to resolve. Chances are, if these more challenging situations come up while you are still a beginner, you may mess up big time. You may feel like a failure.

> Every mistake is an opportunity for growth and you learn through challenges.

But you aren't. I don't know how many times I did the "wrong" thing in conflict resolution and women left in a huff, never to speak to me again. When this happened, I had to forgive myself and remind myself to have the right mindset, which is this: Every mistake is an opportunity for growth and you learn through challenges. They make you a better facilitator.

Additionally, going deeper into your own healing will likewise improve your facilitation skills, particularly with deeper and more intense circle experiences.

Go Deeper in Your Healing

"The wings of transformation are born of patience and struggle."
~ Janet Dickens

Earlier in the book, I talked about growing yourself in order to grow your circle, and now I want to talk about going deeper into your healing, because ultimately the circles that we are talking about are transformational circles. Healing occurs in these circles. They're about women coming in as one person and literally metamorphosing into a whole new person. When they leave, they are transformed for the better.

I've said before that you can only lead your circle as deep as you are personally willing and able to go. Circle is a mirror: whatever happens shows you opportunities for your own healing. If there is a lot of chaos, chances are it's reflecting your own chaos. If women aren't attending, chances are there's something in your space that's lacking. You need to be able to go deeper to look at the energetic blocks or limiting beliefs that are in your space.

Here are seven ways that you can go deeper into your own healing to really grow your circles and to have them evolve and mature.

1. Understand inclusivity.

What we see is that women in circle tend to look the same, act the same, and have the same background, but the power of circle is really in the diversity of the circle. When we have women from different ages, races, ethnicities, and sexual orientations, then we have different perspectives. We begin to develop greater empathy and compassion. We expand our capacity to love. We get to see that we all share the same human experience, the same heart, and we also begin to honor and respect those differences. Coming together despite our differences is ultimately how we create oneness on the planet.

This is really challenging, especially for women like me who grew up with white privilege. Here in the United States, this topic has become even more relevant as women of color are speaking up about their experience with systemic racism and people in the LGBTQ+ community are coming out with their stories of bullying, homophobia and discrimination.

I've had women of color question whether they belong at Sistership Circle, and while my knee jerk reaction was "of course they belong!" I had to take a deeper look at what white privilege is, how I can release my own limited beliefs, and how I can make my circles more inclusive.

GO DEEPER IN YOUR HEALING

I'm still learning and growing every day. I'm not perfect, but I know I'm on the right path.

This level of growth is required to create a safe space for all women.

Every circle is open to *every* woman, regardless of age, race, sexual orientation, gender, and any other qualifier. *You* are a woman and *you belong* here with us, getting healing, celebration, no judgment, and sisterhood.

2. Develop the major archetypes within yourself.

We've covered 4 of the feminine leader archetypes, and there are many more; the more that you can explore these different archetypes that all live within you, the more that you can play your full range and be more fully self expressed as yourself. Developing these archetypes will allow you to develop more of your superpowers and your strengths as a woman and to be able to relate to other women who are stronger in any specific archetype than you are.

3. Allow yourself to be more fully seen.

We can break down the word *intimacy* as "into me see."

How much can you open yourself up to allow others to really see you? Can you take the guard down and stop protecting yourself? Can you let go of the story that someone has to prove themselves trustworthy before you let them in? The most powerful circle leaders are the ones people feel like they could connect with, that they feel safe with, because they are able to be present. They have developed intimacy and they are open and available for a deeper connection.

THE ART OF LEADING CIRCLE

4. Trust your voice and become more visible.

It's an inner game to put yourself out there. To grow your circles, you need to be able to speak up and share about your circles. You also need to become more visible. If you're someone who struggles with putting a picture of yourself up on social media, or you've never done a Facebook Live, chances are there's something for you to uncover deeper within yourself, perhaps healing a part of you probably from childhood who is afraid of being seen. Visibility and promoting your circle is an integral piece you must conquer to be successful and grow your circles.

5. Heal your mother wound.

At the root of the sister wound is the mother wound. In order for us to really create sacred sistership, we need to not only heal our own sister wounds but also that deeper disconnect with the feminine, and with our own mothers.

6. Let go of your "identity" and develop self esteem based on who you *are*, not what you do.

We become so attached to the tasks that we've completed, the accomplishments, what we do in the world; we become attached to an identity, as a CEO, as a mother, as an employee, whatever it is that we base our self worth on according to what we do out there in the world.

But healing this aspect is about developing your self-worth and self-esteem based on your internal qualifications. Understand fully that you matter simply because you are here, that you don't actually need to *do* anything to exist and be a contribution on this planet.

Feeling this truth, trusting and knowing it, is how you will become that open space for women to feel a sense of belonging -- because you feel that belonging within yourself. You *get* that you belong on this planet, not based on your accolades or your job title, but simply because you are a human being.

7. Feel worthy and deserving of receiving.

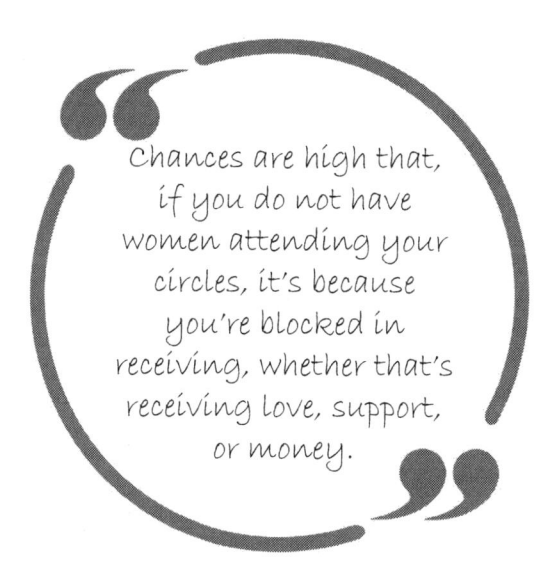

> Chances are high that, if you do not have women attending your circles, it's because you're blocked in receiving, whether that's receiving love, support, or money.

Chances are high that, if you do not have women attending your circles, it's because you're blocked in receiving, whether that's receiving love, support, or money. The more you can really understand that yes, you deserve to receive, you balance out the overgiving. You'll create an opening for more women to come in because you feel like you're worthy of receiving these women into your space. You are worthy of being a circle facilitator.

While we've been focusing on growing your circle, I want to also make a caveat that it's not all about growth all the time. That's unsustainable. Instead of focusing on constant growth, part of being a circle facilitator is also honoring the natural cycle of circle.

Honor the Cycle

"Energy moves in cycles, circles, spirals, vortexes, whirls, pulsations, waves, and rhythms—rarely if ever in simple straight lines."
~ Starhawk

Although it may seem contradictory, one of the biggest blocks to growing your circles is actually your own attachment to women *staying* in your circles. I used to get so upset when someone would leave, unsubscribe from my list, or no longer want to come to my circles. I would take it personally, thinking that I had done something wrong, but the truth is that all life includes endings, and we have to allow people the freedom to come in and out of our lives.

The saying that people are in your life for a reason, a season, or a lifetime is definitely applicable to circle. Constant expansion and growth is also not sustainable. We must allow for the contractions, the

THE ART OF LEADING CIRCLE

times of rest and reflection, and the times of transition. Honoring the seasons and the cycle of life creates more flow in our circles. You must learn to allow the life and death cycles of your circle.

If you are constantly stretching and playing your edge, you are going to be changing and transforming, which means that you are going to attract different women depending on where you are in your life cycle and your own growth. There will be lulls when you are in transition to the next stage of your personal development. The trick is to not panic if, for one month or two, your circle shrinks to half your normal sized gathering. That shrinkage doesn't mean you are going backward. It simply means it's time to take pause, reflect, reevaluate, and make room for what wants to come through next.

There will be women who fall away. There will be women who no longer resonate with your energy if they're not growing with you. This is true for all relationships; what gets in the way of this natural process is our own attachment.

For example, I had an attachment to my high school best friend and I was devastated when we started to drift apart. But, I could see that we were going in different directions and so I had to let her go and trust in our life paths, so now I just love and accept her for exactly where she's at. I have gratitude for the experiences that we had together, but I needed to go through a death ceremony for that relationship. And like we've seen so much throughout this book, *this is all the same with your circles*.

Earlier, I talked about how a short-term circle inevitably ends, and how we need to create intentional space to close the circle.

Here's how to lead a completion ceremony:

HONOR THE CYCLE

Step 1: Designate a final circle, or if it's a retreat, carve out a specific time for a Completion Ceremony.

You need to be intentional about carving out the time, otherwise you can easily step over it and the opportunity is gone.

Step 2: Mention the context and importance of the Completion Ceremony.

Usually, I talk about the life cycle of beginnings and endings, changes of the season, and day and night as the context for completion. I also mention and give permission for women to feel grief around the ending, especially if the group went very deep and feels extremely bonded. This allows women to express themselves and hold nothing back.

Step 3: Have each woman share her celebrations and positive takeaways from the circle.

I always start with the positive. Each woman gets 3-5 minutes to talk about all the highlights from her experience.

Step 4: Have each woman give voice to anything that feels incomplete: any regrets, any sadness, and anything negative, so they don't carry it forward.

I never skip over this part and I urge women to be real and hold nothing back, otherwise it can have a negative impact later if they continue to hold onto any regrets or negativity.

Step 5: Have each woman be acknowledged by at least one other woman.

THE ART OF LEADING CIRCLE

There is nothing more powerful than taking the time for each woman to feel seen, heard, and valued as a circle participant. At Sistership Circle, we use what we call the Acknowledgement Train.

Here's how it goes:

Person A goes first and calls on someone: "Person B, what would you like to be acknowledged for?"

Person B says, "I would like to be acknowledged for _____."

Person A then acknowledges Person B for that.

Person B then calls on someone: "Person C, what would you like to be acknowledged for?"

Each woman continues to call on someone until the last person goes back to acknowledge Person A.

This is a wonderful exercise which makes everyone feel uplifted, connected and complete.

Step 6: Perform a ritual to officially signify the end of the circle.

This can be as simple as blowing out a candle and saying "The circle is now complete!" or you can make up another ritual that energetically closes the container.

One of the most important tools in circle is conscious completion, especially if someone from a long-term circle decides to formally end her participation before the entire group ends. If someone decides to leave, you want to honor their completion and create the space in a ceremony for them to complete their journey with the circle.

HONOR THE CYCLE

The ceremony is where she gets to share all that she received from the circle. She can share anything that feels incomplete, any withholds, and the other women can also each share what they have received from her and what they're celebrating about her. In this way, she gets to close her part in the circle authentically, and the circle remains unbroken.

Imagine if the world had more conscious completion! Instead of an ugly divorce, a couple that was separating could have a beautiful conscious completion ceremony where they get to honor each other, which would then create more peace and a much easier divorce process.

So, if someone leaves your circle, you don't want to have bad blood, you want to make sure that any rifts are repaired and women can freely move on because you've let them go energetically.

When we stay attached to people being in our circle, or we try to manipulate them into staying, we're blocking the flow of energy from allowing the circle to grow. If someone is there who is not meant to be, but you are attached and have convinced her to stay, she's taking up space for someone who actually might be a better match for the circle. Let her go so she can find a new space that's also a better energetic match for her.

As you grow and evolve, you are birthing new circles, shifting and attracting the right women who are in alignment with your soul at any given time. Before we can birth anew, we have to go through the death process of the old.

As we close, I'm going to walk you through a completion process so that you can reflect on what you learned and consider your own next steps to keep flourishing as a circle leader.

THE ART OF LEADING CIRCLE

Featured Facilitator: Natasha Daubney

The call of the Sacred Cycles first came to me as an invitation to deepen with the Earth and in turn, I was drawn to deepen with my body and energy here in the physical world.

As I began to observe and honor the cycles Mama Earth moves through with more awareness, I was able to recognize how I flow through these cycles myself. Through the connection with my womb, I learned how important they were for me to be in my most empowered state and reflect with more ease on what is out of alignment when I'm not in my empowered state. This has been a key piece for me to tap into the energy of the circles I desire to create, and bring to the women in my community, because the circles I lead are a reflection of me.

My journey to building circles that feel magical and draw women in has been up and down, to say the least. I've had full circles and I've had circles where I'm scrambling to conjure up more than one woman. I've invested time, energy, and money, feeling so sure, only to put on a smiling face and bypass my disappointment of not filling my circle thinking next time will be better...

"Life is always trying to initiate us." - Rebecca Campbell

As I reflect back now from a place where I am finally feeling aligned with what I am offering and seeing growth, I can see that this is all a part of my initiation. This is my journey to truly understanding what I WANT to receive from circle and how to create circle so that it blends into my life.

Just like our womb, just like the Earth, life is cyclical, and each and every day we move through the process of life, death, and rebirth. We are never the same from one moment to the next, ever-evolving as we experience what life has designed for us.

HONOR THE CYCLE

Everything I struggled with was trying to call out for me to stop clinging to ideals and to let go of my attachment to being "good," "perfect," and "having it all together." It was my safe way of being, but it created a barrier between myself and others. It created a barrier between who I was and how I brought that into circle.

Living life in a way that compliments my inner rhythms is really important to me, it is the wisdom I love to teach women, and yet I wasn't practicing this with the creation of my circles.

I realized that I wasn't timing my circles for when I wanted to hold them, I was holding them when I thought women would be able to attend. Sometimes I couldn't wait to start, sometimes I couldn't wait for it to be done and dusted.

I realized that I wasn't always honoring the magic and ritual I wanted to work with and my creative power, I was trying to be "mainstream" and not too "out there." Circle felt good, but it wasn't always deeply transformative for me.

I realized that the circles, which were filled and powerful beyond words, were the ones timed for me, with the rituals and magic I wanted for me, with the tools I love to work with when I am on my own in ritual. Only then did the same women start to come back, circle after circle ... because I was finally honoring me.

Life is constantly trying to nudge us toward our death and rebirth, in order to fulfill our soul's desires. It is initiating us every day so we may become the woman we were born to be.

That doesn't mean it will be gentle or comfortable, an initiation is often the opposite because it requires us to cross a threshold from one way of being into another.

To cross that threshold, a piece of us must be surrendered and allowed to die. The piece of ourselves we have been clinging to for the sense of safety it has offered, while in actual fact, it has kept us smaller than we were destined for.

THE ART OF LEADING CIRCLE

I was ready to face the fear, the worry, and the doubts and truly step out as myself. It was both scary and exhilarating to let go of doing what I knew without having any assurance of what will take its place.

And so, I practiced trust.

Trust that the Divine and my soul's guidance would lead me exactly where I needed to go.

Trust that this is the power of circle and this will be my medicine.

Reflect and Take Your Next Step

"We do not learn from experience. We learn from reflecting on experience."
~ John Dewey

At the beginning of this book, I promised that I would give you everything that I had, all of my tips and techniques to effectively fill, lead, and grow your circle. Now, I hope that you go out there (if you haven't already!) and take action to get your circle on the map.

To recap quickly, we've covered:

Some of the most powerful facilitation skills to lead your circles, including:

THE ART OF LEADING CIRCLE

- when to discern between using your outline and using your intuition
- how to structure your circle and create hot topics for discussion
- the balance and integration between the masculine structure and the feminine flow
- four archetypes and their respective super powers to effectively hold space

How to start and fill your circle, including:

- clarifying your *why to lead* so you magnetize the right women to your circle
- committing to a date, time, cost, and venue that feels good for you
- how to effectively share your circle and put the word out there
- the best way to prepare the circle space

And how to grow your circle, including:

- staying consistent with six monthly gatherings
- avoiding burn out with exquisite self-care
- building community that builds on itself
- how to make supplemental income leading circles

Leading transformational circles is truly an art form, and a profound experience.

If you have been inspired by the Sistership Circle vision and mission, I want to take this opportunity to invite you to apply to become one of our licensed Facilitators by doing the Level 1 Certification, the How to Lead Circle Program. What's different about this program is that you get to sit in circle with other leaders and practice all of what we teach

REFLECT AND TAKE YOUR NEXT STEP

you. Plus, you get the coaching and support to break through your limited beliefs and embody your feminine leadership.

As a Sistership Circle facilitator, you get some incredible benefits that you can't find anywhere else. All the benefits you receive from Sistership Circle training can be summed up in two words: Community and Platform.

Imagine having powerful facilitators from all around the world supporting you, women who have your back and celebrate you as you continue to step into your leadership.

Imagine building a movement, together with these women from different walks of life, knowing that you are contributing to one of the most impactful missions of the planet *together*. That we are healing the divide amongst women as we set the example of the new model of feminine leadership, collaborating and co-creating *together*.

This is the Sistership Circle community.

Now imagine having *your* circle posted on an online map, featuring hundreds of other circles from around the world, so when someone comes to the site, they say, "Wow, if all these women are doing this circle thing, I should too!" Imagine that instant credibility as a global leader in the circle movement.

And imagine having all the circle outlines and marketing materials professionally done for you, so that you can focus entirely on gathering women and leading them in circle.

This is the Sistership Circle platform.

THE ART OF LEADING CIRCLE

To really solidify the journey we've been through, take some time to process what you have gained from this book.

What are the top three takeaways you have received?

What are the top three things you can celebrate about *yourself* after finishing the book?

What are the top three fears that are standing in the way of your leading circle, and what are the three strengths you already have to overcome them?

And lastly: what date will you start your first circle, if you have not already done so?

30

Closing

"It always seems impossible until it is done."
~ Nelson Mandela

And so, here at the close, I want to end with something I do at the end of every circle program: a completion ceremony.

Place both your hands on your heart, close your eyes, and take a deep breath.

Breathe in gratitude to be alive on this planet at this unique time, where we have such an incredible opportunity to lead circle.

Breathe in love and celebration of who you are as a feminine leader, growing and expanding yourself to meet your soul's purpose.

THE ART OF LEADING CIRCLE

Breathe in courage and strength to take action despite any fears that arise, so that you can fulfill your desires and dreams.

In celebration of you, I want to end with a beam: I see you, I hear you, I value *you*, sister.

Now go out there and gather the women and lead them in circle. They are waiting for you.

Resource Section

Read one of the most influential books on circle: *Moving Toward the Millionth Circle: Energizing the Global Women's Movement*, by Jean Shinoda Bolen, Conari Press, 2013.

Read one of the most inspiring books on sisterhood: *Mighty Be Our Powers: How Sisterhood, Prayer, and Sex Changed a Nation at War*, by Leymah Gbowee, Beast Books; First Trade Paper Ed edition, 2013.

Get the Meditations For Circle (and scripts) available in the Sistership Circle store: https://sistershipcircle.com/shop

Get the Playsheets in our Art of Leading Circle Startup Kit: https://sistershipcircle.com/shop

Find out your Circle Leader Archetype: https://sistershipcircle.com/archetype-quiz/

Get the Women's Circle Ritual Handbooks: https://sistershipcircle.com/shop

Watch Brene Brown video on The Power of Vulnerability: https://www.ted.com/talks/brene_brown_the_power_of_vulnerability

Read one of the most influential books on community building: *The Different Drum: Community Making and Peace*, by M Scott Peck, M.D. New York; Simon & Schuster, 1987.

THE ART OF LEADING CIRCLE

Learn more about the Karpman Drama triangle: https://sistershipcircle.com/the-karpman-drama-triangle-in-circle/

Read *The Presence Process: A Journey Into Present Moment Awareness*, by Michael Brown, Namaste Publishing, 2010.

Learn more about racial equity with Trudi Lebron: https://www.trudilebron.com/

Read one of the best articles on the Mother Wound by Bethany Webster: https://www.bethanywebster.com/why-its-crucial-for-women-to-heal-the-mother-wound/

Connect with our Community at Sistership Circle

Connect on social media

Our community Facebook Group: https://www.facebook.com/groups/sistershipcircle

Instagram: https://www.instagram.com/sistershipcircle

Sit in circle (locally or virtually)

Find a circle led by one of our certified facilitators: https://sistershipcircle.com/event

Become a Certified Sistership Circle Facilitator

If you feel inspired by our mission and want to join the movement, your first step is to take the How to Lead Circle program.

Learn more at: https://sistershipcircle.com/become-a-facilitator

About the Author

Tanya Lynn is a "strategic activator" — gifted at coaching women to soar to new heights by putting together a plan that maximizes their talents and strengths and taking bold, courageous actions to fulfill on their intentions.

Tanya is the visionary CEO behind Sistership Circle, an international organization providing a platform for circles and leadership training. She started training facilitators in 2014 to use her proven 12-week circle program "The Experience" based on her bestselling book "Open Your Heart: How to be a New Generation Feminine Leader" and has empowered thousands of women to start and grow their circles.

She is a respected leader in the industry from clients and colleagues alike because she's the real deal, living and breathing her work.

She believes that the new model of feminine leadership is not about hierarchies of power but about circles of collaboration. For us to become true leaders, we must embrace our sisters as our allies and give one another permission to shine.

Tanya lives in Encinitas, CA with her husband Brent (co-founder of Sistership Circle), their two daughters Kali and Summer, and cat Simba.

Made in the USA
Columbia, SC
23 August 2023